Crystallization-Study
of the
Psalms

Volume One

Witness Lee

The Holy Word for Morning Revival

Living Stream Ministry

Anaheim, CA • www.lsm.org

First Edition, July 2011.

ISBN 978-0-7363-4830-0

Published by

Living Stream Ministry

2431 W. La Palma Ave., Anaheim, CA 92801 U.S.A.

P. O. Box 2121, Anaheim, CA 92814 U.S.A.

Printed in the United States of America

11 12 13 14 / 5 4 3 2 1

Contents

Preface

1. This book is intended as an aid to believers in developing a daily time of morning revival with the Lord in His word. At the same time, it provides a limited review of the summer training held July 4-9, 2011, in Anaheim, California, on the "Crystallization-study of the Psalms." Through intimate contact with the Lord in His word, the believers can be constituted with life and truth and thereby equipped to prophesy in the meetings of the church unto the building up of the Body of Christ.

2. The entire content of this book is taken from *Crystallization-study Outlines: The Psalms (1)*, the text and footnotes of the Recovery Version of the Bible, selections from the writings of Witness Lee and Watchman Nee, and *Hymns*, all of which are published by Living Stream Ministry.

3. The book is divided into weeks. One training message is covered per week. Each week presents first the message outline, followed by six daily portions, a hymn, and then some space for writing. The training outline has been divided into days, corresponding to the six daily portions. Each daily portion covers certain points and begins with a section entitled "Morning Nourishment." This section contains selected verses and a short reading that can provide rich spiritual nourishment through intimate fellowship with the Lord. The "Morning Nourishment" is followed by a section entitled "Today's Reading," a longer portion of ministry related to the day's main points. Each day's portion concludes with a short list of references for further reading and some space for the saints to make notes concerning their spiritual inspiration, enlightenment, and enjoyment to serve as a reminder of what they have received of the Lord that day.

4. The space provided at the end of each week is for composing a short prophecy. This prophecy can be composed by considering all of our daily notes, the "harvest" of our inspirations during the week, and preparing a main point with

some sub-points to be spoken in the church meetings for the organic building up of the Body of Christ.

5. Following the last week in this volume, we have provided reading schedules for both the Old and New Testaments in the Recovery Version with footnotes. These schedules are arranged so that one can read through both the Old and New Testaments of the Recovery Version with footnotes in two years.

6. As a practical aid to the saints' feeding on the Word throughout the day, we have provided verse cards at the end of the volume, which correspond to each day's scripture reading. These may be cut out and carried along as a source of spiritual enlightenment and nourishment in the saints' daily lives.

7. *Crystallization-study Outlines: The Psalms (1)* was compiled by Living Stream Ministry from the writings of Witness Lee and Watchman Nee. The outlines, footnotes, and cross-references in the Recovery Version of the Bible are by Witness Lee. All of the other references cited in this publication are from the published ministry of Witness Lee and Watchman Nee.

Summer Training
(July 4-9, 2011)

CRYSTALLIZATION-STUDY
OF THE PSALMS

Banners:

The central thought of the book of Psalms
is Christ, as revealed in plain words,
and the church as the house of God and
the city of God for His kingdom,
as typified by the temple and by the city of Jerusalem.

It is by Christ's wonderful shepherding
and by our entering into this shepherding
that the Body of Christ will be built up
with His redeemed and regenerated ones
and that the bride will be prepared
for Him to return as the King in the next age
in the manifestation of His kingdom.

If we have an affectionate love for the Lord Jesus,
our tongue will be the pen of a ready writer,
ready to write our love for Him and our praise to Him
with our experience and enjoyment of Him
according to all that He is.

At His second coming,
Christ will take possession of the earth
and will establish God's kingdom on earth,
spreading the kingdom by Himself as the flowing river,
recovering the earth by watering,
and satisfying the thirsty ones with living water.

The Central Thought of the Book of Psalms

Scripture Reading: Psa. 2:6-9; 27:4; 36:8-9; 48:1-2; 72:8; 22:27

Day 1   I. The Psalms are fully Christ centered; Christ is not only the centrality but also the universality of the Psalms (Luke 24:44).

II. The central thought of the book of Psalms is Christ, as revealed in plain words, and the church as the house of God and the city of God for His kingdom, as typified by the temple and by the city of Jerusalem (2:6-9; 26:8; 27:4; 46:4):

A. The spirit, the reality, the characteristic, of the divine revelation in the book of Psalms is Christ as the centrality and universality of the eternal economy of God (2:6-9):

     1. For this, Christ is first the embodiment of the Triune God (Col. 2:9), then the house, the habitation, of God (signified by the temple—John 2:19-21), the kingdom of God (signified by the city of Jerusalem—Luke 17:21; Rev. 22:3b), and the Ruler of the entire earth from the house of God and in the kingdom of God (Dan. 2:34-35).

     2. Christ is therefore all in all in the entire universe (Eph. 1:23; Col. 3:11).

B. The picture given in the book of Psalms is the same as that portrayed by the entire Bible: Christ, the church, and the reigning of Christ over the whole earth with the New Jerusalem as the center (Matt. 16:16, 18; Rev. 21:1-3, 24).

C. The particular point related to the divine revelation in the Psalms is that such a high revelation is prophesied in the expressions of the sentiments of the ancient godly saints.

D. The consummation of the divine revelation is the city of New Jerusalem as a sign of the habitation, the tabernacle, of God, through which the processed and consummated Triune God will be manifested and expressed in the all-inclusive Christ and

will reign on the new earth in the new universe for
eternity (Rev. 21:1-3).

E. The five books of the Psalms are arranged in the same
progressive way as the entire Bible is arranged:

1. From the first book of the Psalms to the fifth
book, the revelation progresses higher and
higher; the fifth book is filled with the psalmists' praising of God.

2. The central thought in this progressive revelation is that God is embodied in Christ, Christ
is in His Body, and His Body is God's house
and God's city for God's kingdom over the
earth (Col. 2:9; Eph. 1:22-23; 2:19; Rev. 11:15).

Day 2 III. **The book of Psalms covers four main points in
a wonderful sequence: Christ—house—city—
earth (2:6-7; 27:4; 48:2; 72:8):**

A. In the Psalms we see the details concerning the all-
inclusive Christ in God's eternal economy:

1. Christ in His divinity (45:6; Heb. 1:8).

2. Christ in His incarnation (Psa. 8:4; Heb. 2:6).

3. Christ in His humanity (Psa. 8:4; Heb. 2:6).

4. Christ in His human living (Psa. 16:1-8).

5. Christ in His death (22:1-21).

6. Christ in His resurrection (2:7; 16:10; 22:22;
Heb. 2:12; Acts 2:25-32; 13:33-37).

7. Christ in His ascension (Psa. 68:18; Eph. 4:8).

8. Christ in His exaltation (Psa. 80:17; 110:1).

9. Christ in His being crowned (8:5; Heb. 2:9).

10. Christ in His enthronement (Psa. 2:6).

11. Christ in His dominion, kingship, and authority (v. 8; 8:6; 47:2; 72:8).

12. Christ in His priesthood (110:4).

13. Christ in His fighting (vv. 5-6; 45:3-5).

14. Christ in His victory (110:5-6).

15. Christ in His indwelling (22:22).

16. Christ in His shepherding (23).

17. Christ as the stone for the building (118:22).

18. Christ in His coming (72; 96; 110).

19. Christ in His reigning (93—101).

Day 3

B. The Psalms reveal many aspects of the church as God's house, such as:
1. God's dwelling (68:18; 84:1).
2. The ground, the site (24:3; 68:16; 76:2).
3. Its foundation (87:1).
4. The place of God's presence, which is God's glory (26:8; 27:4; 29:9).
5. The place of revelation (73:17).
6. The saints' desire (84:2, 10).
7. Its loveliness (v. 1).
8. The place where we may be planted, flourish, and bear fruit (92:13-14).
9. The place of springs (87:7).
10. The place of worship (99:9).
11. The place where God is our portion (73:26).
12. The place where we are mingled with God (92:10).

Day 4

C. The Psalms reveal aspects of the church as the city, such as:
1. It is the city of the great King (48:2).
2. There is a river with streams within it (46:4).
3. God is in the midst of the city (v. 5).
4. It is God's holy mountain (48:1).
5. It is beautiful in elevation and the joy of the whole earth (v. 2).
6. It is the perfection of beauty (50:2).
7. It is the goal of God's good pleasure (51:18).
8. It is the salvation of God's people (53:6).
9. It is God's resting place forever (132:14).
10. The city is built up by the Lord (147:2).
11. The Lord blesses others from the city (134:3).
12. The Lord is blessed from the city (135:21).

Day 5 & Day 6

D. Various aspects of the earth are also seen in the Psalms, such as:
1. The earth has been given to Christ as an inheritance (2:8).
2. The Lord's name will be excellent in all the earth (8:1).
3. The earth and its fullness are the Lord's (24:1).

4. Christ will come back to take the earth (96:13).
5. Christ will reign over the earth (72:8).
6. The earth will return to Christ (22:27).
7. The earth will remember Christ (v. 27).
8. The earth will worship Christ (vv. 27, 29).
9. The earth will praise Christ (98:4).
10. The whole earth will be filled with God's glory (72:19).

IV. **The book of Psalms reveals that the earth is the ultimate intention of God's desire (8:1, 9):**

A. The Psalms show us that God's intention is to recover His title, His legal rights, over the whole earth through Christ in the church as the house and the city (2:6-8; 36:8-9; 48:2; 72:8).

B. God must conquer the earth, recover the earth, and bring the earth back under His rightful rule (8:1, 9); this is why the Lord taught us to pray, "Your kingdom come; Your will be done, as in heaven, so also on earth" (Matt. 6:10).

C. God's purpose is to express Himself in a corporate way, and the key to the fulfillment of God's purpose is the building up of the church; without the church as the house and the city, there is no beachhead for the Lord to come back and recover the earth (16:18; Eph. 3:9-11; 4:16; Rev. 11:15).

D. When the church is enlarged from the house to the city for the recovery of the earth, God's purpose will be fulfilled, and we will declare, "O Jehovah our Lord, / How excellent is Your name / In all the earth!" (Psa. 8:9).

Morning Nourishment

Luke 24:44	And He said to them, These are My words which I spoke to you while I was still with you, that all the things written in the Law of Moses and the Prophets and Psalms concerning Me must be fulfilled.
Psa. 2:6-7	But I have installed My King upon Zion, My holy mountain. I will recount the decree of Jehovah; He said to Me: You are My Son; today I have begotten You.

We need to enter into the right way to understand all of the psalms one by one....The book of Psalms, in the proper understanding, is centered on Christ. The Psalms are fully Christ-centered. Christ is not only the centrality but also the universality of the Psalms. I believe that the Lord has given us the proper and particular way to study, to know, and to interpret the Psalms.

Apparently, according to the human concept, all the Psalms are the expressions of the sentiments, feelings, and impressions of godly men who were intimately close to God.

Actually, according to the divine concept, the central thought of the book of Psalms is Christ, as revealed in plain words (Luke 24:44), and the church as the house of God and the city of God for His kingdom, as typified by the temple and the city of Jerusalem. (*Life-study of the Psalms*, pp. 127, 9)

Today's Reading

Revelation 19:10 says that the spirit of the prophecy of the book of Revelation is the testimony of Jesus. Based upon this principle we can say that the spirit, the reality, the characteristic, of the divine revelation in the book of Psalms is Christ (Luke 24:44) as the centrality and universality of the eternal economy of God. For this, He is firstly the embodiment of the Triune God, then the house, the habitation, of God (signified by the temple), the kingdom of God (signified by the city of Jerusalem), and the Ruler of the entire earth from the house of God and in the kingdom of God. Thus, He is all in all in the entire universe....The only particular point of the divine revelation in the book of Psalms is that such a high revelation, even the highest peak of the divine revelation, is prophesied in the expressions of the sentiments of the ancient godly saints. So it is mixed with their comfort in sufferings and the cultivation of godliness, yet the center and the reality, the spirit, of this highest revelation is not the comfort in sufferings nor the cultivation of godliness. It is the Christ of God, who is all in all according to God's desire and for God's good pleasure.

The consummation of this highest divine revelation is the city of New Jerusalem as a sign of the habitation, the tabernacle, of God (Rev. 21:1-3), through which the Triune God is manifested and expressed in the all-inclusive Christ.

God desires to have an organic habitation on earth, and this habitation is the aggregate of the living saints gained by God through the terminating death and germinating resurrection of the all-inclusive Christ. They will be the eternal manifestation and expression of the processed and consummated Triune God, and He will be everything to them in His all-inclusive Christ. The Triune God will reign on the new earth through such an organism in the new universe. This is the spirit, the extract, of the book of Psalms.

The entire revelation of the Bible is progressive,... [proceeding] higher and higher from Genesis to its peak in Revelation. Genesis 1 speaks of God's creation, but Revelation 22 speaks of the New Jerusalem. God's creation is somewhat easy to understand, but the sign of the New Jerusalem is a great mystery.

The five books of the Psalms were arranged in the same progressive way as the entire Bible was arranged. From the first book of the Psalms to the fifth book, the revelation proceeds higher and higher. The fifth book is full of the psalmists' praising of God. God is embodied in Christ, Christ is in His Body, and His Body is God's house and God's city for God's kingdom. This is all for God's economy. The central thought of the book of Psalms is Christ and the church as the house of God and the city of God for His kingdom. (*Life-study of the Psalms*, pp. 512-513, 32)

Further Reading: Life-study of the Psalms, msgs. 1-2

Enlightenment and inspiration: _____

_____

_____

Morning Nourishment

Psa. What is mortal man, that You remember him, and the
8:4-6 son of man, that You visit him? You have made Him a
little lower than angels and have crowned Him with
glory and honor. For You have caused Him to rule
over the works of Your hands; You have put all things
under His feet.

[May we all be] deeply impressed with these four words: *Christ,
house, city, earth.* Let us forget about the negative [word], the *law.*
We must always remember God's Christ, the house of God, the city
of God, and the earth....The entire book of the Psalms just covers
these main points in a wonderful sequence. We have also seen that
the picture given to us by the book of Psalms is exactly the same
as that portrayed by the entire Bible. The whole Bible reveals
only Christ, then the church, and then the reigning of Christ over
the whole earth with the New Jerusalem as the center.

The main psalms concerning Christ are Psalms 2, 8, 16, 22, 23,
24, 45, 68, 80, 91, 110, and 118.

These are just the main aspects; there are many details which
could be filled in. It is clear that through the Psalms we can know
Christ much better than through the New Testament. (*Christ
and the Church Revealed and Typified in the Psalms,* pp. 225-226)

Today's Reading

The Psalms...[reveal] how the Holy Spirit turned the psalmists from the law, which they loved and tried to keep, to Christ, of
whom they did not have any idea. The psalmists were right in
seeking after God, but they were not right in making the law of
God the goal of their seeking. They needed to be turned in their
seeking from the law to Christ. Whereas the law is a side line in
the Scriptures, Christ, the tree of life, is the main line.

Next, the Psalms ministers to the Bible readers, in their igno-
rant seeking of God, the all-inclusive Christ in God's economy. It is
not adequate for us to be turned from the law to Christ; we also
need to know that Christ is the center and the circumference, the
hub and the rim, of God's eternal economy. This means that in

God's eternal economy Christ is everything. He is the centrality and He is also the universality. We need to study the Psalms in order to learn the details concerning this all-inclusive Christ in God's eternal economy. (*Life-study of Job,* pp. 195-196)

From the human standpoint, we may say that the center and content of all the psalms are the experiences of the saints concerning God's mercy, kindness, love, faithfulness, power, and glory. They experienced so much of God's goodness that they praised God with all these aspects of their experience of God. This is the human concept; this is the human point of view. But according to the divine concept and the divine point of view, the center and content of all the praises are Christ, the house, and the city of God. Christ is the center, and the church, typified by the house and the city, is also the center. Christ and the church are the center and content of all the praises of the Psalms. Therefore, in all our praises we must have the sentiments and impressions gathered from our experience; yet in all our praises we must have Christ and the church as the center and the content.

Christian teachers always declare that the Psalms are sweet and comforting....It is true that the Psalms are indeed a comfort, but if we merely apply the Psalms for our comfort, we fail greatly and come far short of their intent. The Psalms were not written in this way; they were written as praise to God with Christ as the center. Christ Himself told His disciples that in the books of Moses, in the Prophets, and in the Psalms, many things were written concerning Him (Luke 24:44). It is a great pity that so many Christians merely apply the Psalms for comfort. Very few apply the Psalms for the experience of Christ.

It is good to be mindful of the Lord's goodness and mercy toward us, but our praises must be Christ-centered and church-centered. (*Christ and the Church Revealed and Typified in the Psalms,* pp. 10-11)

Further Reading: Christ and the Church Revealed and Typified in the Psalms, ch. 1; *Life-study of Job,* msg. 36

Enlightenment and inspiration: _____

_____

_____

_____

Morning Nourishment

Psa. One thing I have asked from Jehovah; that do I seek:
27:4 to dwell in the house of Jehovah all the days of my
life, to behold the beauty of Jehovah, and to inquire in
His temple.
84:1 How lovely are Your tabernacles, O Jehovah of hosts!

The Lord will recover the earth, the earth which is now usurped
by the enemy. The secret is in Psalm 24. The earth is the Lord's; so
the Lord has the right, the title, to the earth. He realizes this right
by the "mountain." The mountain is the key, the steppingstone,
for the Lord's recovery of the earth. Upon this mountain is the
house, and the house is built up with the brothers. The brothers
were brought forth by the resurrection of Christ, and the resurrection issued from His crucifixion. Before His crucifixion there
was His wonderful life on this earth, a life which issued from His
incarnation. Thus, we have all these major steps leading up to
God's recovery of the earth: His incarnation in Psalm 8, His human
living in Psalm 16, His crucifixion and resurrection in Psalm 22
(His resurrection is also mentioned or implied in Psalms 2, 8, and
16), His brothers in Psalm 22, His house in Psalm 23, and eventually the mountain on the earth in Psalm 24. (*Christ and the
Church Revealed and Typified in the Psalms*, p. 62)

Today's Reading

The main point of the first book, Psalms 1—41, is that God's
intention is to turn the seeking saints from the law to Christ in
order that they may enjoy the house of God. I believe that by now
we have all turned to Christ....The saints experience and enjoy
God through Christ, especially in the house and the city of God.

The subject of the first psalm is the law. But immediately in
the second psalm, the subject is changed from the law to Christ.
Hallelujah! Beginning with Psalm 2 we have...six psalms of
Christ, ending with Psalm 24. But however much we appreciate
the preciousness of Christ, we must realize that Christ is not the
consummation. Christ is for the house; Christ is for the church. In
Matthew 16, when Peter saw Christ by the Father's revelation,

the Lord immediately directed his attention to the church: "I *also* say to you that you are Peter, and upon this rock I will build My *church*" (v. 18). Here in the Psalms we first have the law, according to the human, natural, religious concept of the saints. But God turned the saints to Christ. Then we have Christ revealed, portrayed, and detailed in Psalms 2, 8, 16, 22, 23, and 24. We must repeat again and again these psalms about the preciousness of Christ. But in this section, from Psalm 2 to Psalm 24, we have very little mentioned of the house. Indeed, the house is mentioned in these psalms (see 5:7; 11:4; and 18:6), but it is not emphasized. These few references to the house speak only of such matters as coming into His house, praising God in His temple, and prayer being heard in the temple. But following Psalm 24, from Psalms 25 to 41, the house is set forth in a richer way. In all these seventeen psalms, Christ is not often mentioned, but the house is repeatedly emphasized. The main thing in this section is the house. There is reference after reference to the house. Oh, the house, the house, for the enjoyment of God! It is in this section that the wonderful verse is found: "Taste and see that Jehovah is good" (34:8). But where may we taste Him? In the house! We can only taste God in His house.

In Psalm 1 the law is everything. But immediately, the Spirit changes the subject to Christ. Then, from Psalms 2 to 24, Christ is richly and strongly presented. Yet, even in these psalms, the law is still not absolutely abandoned. But when we come to Psalms 25 to 41, it is rather difficult to find a single verse concerning the law. I cannot find one. The law is in Psalm 1, but in Psalms 2 to 24 Christ becomes the main figure, and the law is on its way out. Then, in Psalms 25 to 41, the law is over, and the house of God becomes the main figure. We have turned from the law to Christ, and Christ has brought us to the house....Hallelujah for God's house! (*Christ and the Church Revealed and Typified in the Psalms,* pp. 62-64)

Further Reading: Life-study of the Psalms, msg. 12; *Christ and the Church Revealed and Typified in the Psalms,* ch. 6

Enlightenment and inspiration: _____

_____

_____

Morning Nourishment

Psa. Great is Jehovah, and much to be praised in the city
48:1-2 of our God, in His holy mountain. Beautiful in elevation, the joy of the whole earth, is Mount Zion, the
sides of the north, the city of the great King.

We have seen the aspects of Christ and the church as the
house in the Psalms; now let us consider the aspects of the church
as the *city*. These are even more wonderful.

The main psalms concerning the city are Psalms 46, 48, 68, 87,
122, 126, 132, 133, 134, 137, 146, 147, and 149.

When we put all these verses together, we see how wonderful
this city is. Comparing the aspects of the city with the aspects of
the house, we see the difference. The main aspects of the house
speak of God's presence, whereas the principal aspects of the city
bespeak God's authority, God's ruling power, God's reigning. Hence,
the house is for the expression of God, and the city is for the
dominion of God. The house and the city of God fulfill the purpose of God in the creation of man as expressed in Genesis 1:26:
"God said, Let Us make man in Our image, according to Our likeness; and let them have dominion." The image is for the expression, and the dominion is for the authority. Eventually, through
Christ and with Christ we have the house for God's presence, as
God's expression, and we have the city for God's authority, as God's
dominion. (*Christ and the Church Revealed and Typified in the
Psalms*, pp. 229-231)

Today's Reading

God's eternal purpose is fulfilled by the house and the city. In
the house God is a Father, and in the city God is a King. Both the
house and the city are the church, or we may say, the local
churches. A local church, in one sense, must be the house of God,
and in another sense it must also be the city of God.

A city is much stronger and larger than a house. Therefore, we
say that when the house is enlarged, it becomes the city, just as
the New Jerusalem. We are told that in the New Jerusalem there
will be no temple (Rev. 21:22), no house, but just the city. It is

because the entire city of the New Jerusalem is the enlargement of the temple. The temple enlarged becomes the city. It is larger, stronger, and safer than the house.

We can apply the principle of the house and the city to the local churches in this way: If the presence of God is among us, if when people come to our meeting, they worship and say, "God indeed is among you," this is the house. If, on the other hand, when people come among us and realize that there is not only the presence of God but some kind of divine rule and authority, this is not only the house but the house with the city.

Sometimes in a local church we sense the presence of God but not much of God's authority. We sense that God is among them, but that on the other hand there is a shortage of divine order. That means that in that local church there is the reality of the house but not much of the city. In other churches we sense not only the presence of God but also something of divine government and heavenly authority. That is the city. If a local church is in this kind of situation, that church is considerably stronger and safer. It is more elevated, more established, and more enlarged. It is not only the house but the house with the city.

By looking into all these aspects of Christ, the house, and the city as presented in the Psalms, we see how wonderful Christ is, how marvelous the house is, and how glorious and terrifying the city is!

Either for Christ to gain the earth, or for the earth to turn and worship Christ, both are through the city. Christ gains the earth and rules over the earth through the city, because He will be in the city. Then the earth will turn to Christ, remember Christ, worship Christ, and praise Christ—all through the city. The city is for the earth. (*Christ and the Church Revealed and Typified in the Psalms,* pp. 231-232)

Further Reading: Christ and the Church Revealed and Typified in the Psalms, chs. 8-9; *The Recovery of God's House and God's City,* ch. 8

Enlightenment and inspiration: _____

_____

_____

_____

Morning Nourishment

Psa. All the ends of the earth will remember and return to
22:27-29 Jehovah, and all families of the nations will worship
before You; for the kingdom is Jehovah's, and He
rules among the nations. All the flourishing of the
earth will eat and worship...

Now let us consider briefly the aspects of the earth as seen in
the Psalms. The word *earth* appears about one hundred ninety
times altogether in the Psalms.

The main psalms concerning the earth are Psalms 47, 68, 72,
89, 145, 146, 148, and 149.

God's purpose in the entire universe is to express Himself in a
corporate way, not just to express Himself through you or me or
some other individual. This is what the enemy opposes and seeks
to frustrate more than anything else. The problem on the earth
today is headed up in the enemy's frustration to God's fulfillment
of His purpose. The earth became and still is a real frustration to
God. With God's will there is no problem in heaven, but there is a
real problem on this earth (Matt. 6:10). With many Christians
there is a religious concept concerning heaven, which causes
them to continually consider heaven and their going to that place.
But God's concern is for the earth; the earth is His desire. We
would like to go to heaven, but He would like to come to earth.
Eventually, the New Jerusalem will come down out of heaven
(Rev. 21:2). (*Christ and the Church Revealed and Typified in the
Psalms,* pp. 232-233)

Today's Reading

God's problem is now on this earth, which is under Satan's
usurping hand. God's enemy is still usurping the earth to frustrate God's purpose; hence, the struggle between God and Satan
is over this earth. The key to this struggle is humanity. If God
could gain humanity, He would win. If Satan could keep humanity in his hand, he would win. Humanity today is also a problem to
God; so out of humanity God is building up a church. The church,
a building of Christ in humanity, is the key for God to win the

victory. If God today could obtain a church, it is certain that He would have the victory. The Lord has ascended, two thousand years have passed, and still He has not come back. The reason He has not returned is that the church is not ready. Today God has not yet obtained the key, the church that is built up with Christ in humanity.

The Psalms show us that God's intention is to recover His title, His legal rights, over the whole earth through Christ in the church, through Christ in the house, through Christ in the city. Hence, there is the need of the holy mountain of Zion. We not only need Christ, but Christ in Zion, Christ in the holy mountain. Thus, we have seen that the beachhead, the steppingstone, for God to take over the earth is the church. The building up of the church is not a small matter; it is the key to God's purpose. This is His work; it is not ours, and we have no ambition in this affair. But we are burdened today that God must have His key. Without the house, without the city, there is no beachhead for God to launch back and recover the earth.

In past years and even at the present time we have seen that wherever and whenever there is a real expression of God, there we find God's presence, and there we sense God's anointing. God honors such an expression so greatly because it is the key for the fulfillment of His purpose on earth. He needs a church, a proper church. He needs a house and even a city that He may consider as a steppingstone for Him to return. His full and longing desire is to step onto the earth, but there is as yet no steppingstone; there is no place where He may put His feet. He yearns to recover the entire earth from the usurping hand of the serpent, but without a beachhead established here, it is difficult for Him to accomplish it. He is waiting for a built-up church here and there in so many cities on this earth. (*Christ and the Church Revealed and Typified in the Psalms,* pp. 233-234)

Further Reading: Christ and the Church Revealed and Typified in the Psalms, chs. 17-18

Enlightenment and inspiration: _____

_____

_____

Morning Nourishment

Psa.   O Jehovah our Lord, how excellent is Your name in
8:1-2   all the earth, You who have set Your glory over the
        heavens! Out of the mouths of babes and sucklings
        You have established strength because of Your adver-
        saries, to stop the enemy and the avenger.
    9   O Jehovah our Lord, how excellent is Your name in
        all the earth!

All five books of the Psalms show us that the earth is the
ultimate intention of God's desire. He must conquer the earth,
recover the earth, and bring it back under His rightful rule. That
is why the Lord taught us to pray in Matthew 6:9-10, "Your will be
done, as in heaven, so also on earth." But His will is not yet done
on the earth. That is why He taught us to pray, "Your name be
sanctified." But His name is not yet sanctified on earth. That is
why He taught us to pray, "Your kingdom come." But His kingdom
has not yet come. Psalm 8 tells us, "O Jehovah our Lord, / How
excellent is Your name / In all the earth!" But His name is still not
excellent in all the earth. God is waiting for the building up of the
local churches. When He has this, His name will be sanctified, His
kingdom will come, His will will be done on earth as in heaven,
and His name will be excellent in all the earth. The building up
of the local churches is a tremendous matter. (*Christ and the
Church Revealed and Typified in the Psalms*, p. 234)

Today's Reading

In the four or five centuries since the Reformation, the Lord
has recovered many things. He has fully recovered the preaching
of the gospel. From the beginning of the last century to about
1930, the gospel was brought to nearly every corner of the earth.
Wherever you go today, in any leading city, there the gospel is
preached, and there are a number of believers. The Lord has
spent much time to spread His gospel throughout the earth and
to raise up so many believers. Now, in such a situation, what more
must the Lord recover? Undoubtedly, He must recover the practical building up of His local churches in many places with so many

believers as the materials. It is entirely reasonable to arrive at such a conclusion. In this day, before His soon coming, He must have such a building on this earth, at least in all the leading cities. But where is the building? Is it in so many small free groups, denominations, and organizations? Certainly not. It is in the local churches that He is recovering the practical building for His coming back.

We are living today in a very crucial time. We are standing at an extremely strategic point in history. The issue of God's work on the earth today is tremendous. May the Lord be merciful to us and grant us His grace so that we may go on with Him. May He open our eyes to see and appreciate His recovery. We appreciate other works which are being done for the Lord, but the unique, strategic work of the Lord today is the practical building up of the local churches in the leading cities of this earth. After a few years you will see what will come forth all over this earth. The Lord will honor this move. He must have the building up of the house and the city so that He may recover the entire earth. This is our burden. For this reason we have spent so much time studying the Psalms. There is not one book, even in the New Testament, which reveals these things so clearly as the Psalms. The local churches are the steppingstone, the beachhead, for Him to take the earth and fulfill His purpose. He will certainly do it. How glorious this will be! What a wonderful experience we will have at that time!

The more we pray-read the Psalms, the more we see how good it is that God has turned us from the law to Christ, that He has brought us from Christ to the house, that we may be enlarged from the house to the city, and that from the city He is recovering the whole earth. Then God's purpose will be fulfilled. Then we will all say, "O Jehovah our Lord, / How excellent is Your name / In all the earth. Hallelujah!" (*Christ and the Church Revealed and Typified in the Psalms,* pp. 234-235)

Further Reading: Christ and the Church Revealed and Typified in the Psalms, chs. 22-24

Enlightenment and inspiration: _____

_____

_____

_____

Hymns, #1224

1 We from the law to Christ have turned;
   To trust in Him by grace we've learned.
   And since His glory we've discerned
      We only care for Christ!

      We only care for Christ!
      We only care for Christ!
      And since His glory we've discerned
      We only care for Christ!

2 Christ brings us to God's house to dwell,
   Where all day long His praises swell.
   O hallelujah! None can tell
      How lovely is God's house!

      How lovely is God's house!
      How lovely is God's house!
      O hallelujah! None can tell
      How lovely is God's house!

3 The house enlarged the city is;
   The joy of all the nations 'tis,
   The place for God to rule is this
      On Zion's holy hill.

      On Zion's holy hill,
      On Zion's holy hill,
      The place for God to rule is this
      On Zion's holy hill.

4 From Zion Christ will take the earth
   And reign and fill its souls with mirth.
   All nations will proclaim His worth,
      Break forth and sing for joy.

      Break forth and sing for joy,
      Break forth and sing for joy,
      All nations will proclaim His worth,
      Break forth and sing for joy.

5 Christ—house—the city—earth, we see;
   Thus God's great plan fulfilled will be.
   O brothers, let us utterly
      Be one with Him for this.

      Be one with Him for this,
      Be one with Him for this,
      O brothers, let us utterly
      Be one with Him for this.

Composition for prophecy with main point and sub-points: _____

The Revelation concerning Christ in God's Economy

Scripture Reading: Psa. 2

Day 1   I. In our study of the Psalms, we need to realize that the spirit of the Bible is to exalt Christ (Col. 1:15-19):

A. The spirit of the Bible exalts the Christ ordained by God to have the first place in the old creation, in the new creation, in the Body of Christ, and in everything (Matt. 17:5; Col. 1:18).

B. Since Christ has the first place in all things, we must give Him the first place in our being and in all that we do (v. 18; Rev. 2:4).

C. Psalm 2 is according to the divine concept of exalting Christ; in Psalm 2 Christ is exalted as the center of the economy of God.

II. Psalm 2 is God's speaking, God's declaration, God's proclamation, concerning Christ as the center of His economy (vv. 6, 8):

A. The word *economy* is not in Psalm 2, but the revelation and reality of God's economy are there.

B. The King and the kingdom in Psalm 2 show us the economy of God (vv. 6, 8-9):

1. For God to have a King is for the fulfilling of His economy (v. 6).

2. Christ's kingdom will be a great kingdom of all the nations, covering the entire earth; His kingdom will be everywhere to include everyone (vv. 8-9; 22:28; Dan. 7:14).

Day 2   C. Psalm 2 reveals the steps of Christ in God's economy, beginning from His being anointed in eternity in His divinity (v. 2) and continuing with His resurrection (implying His death also—v. 7; cf. Acts 13:33), His ascension (Psa. 2:6), His setting up His universal kingdom (Rev. 11:15) with the nations as His inheritance and the ends of the earth as His possession (Psa. 2:8), and His ruling the nations with an iron rod (v. 9).

III. **We need to see the divine revelation of Christ in God's economy in Psalm 2:**

A. Verses 1 through 3 predict the opposition of the world rulers to Christ; the fulfillment of these verses began with Herod and Pontius Pilate and will conclude with Antichrist (Acts 4:25-28; Rev. 19:19).

B. In Psalm 2:2 God came in to declare that Christ was His Anointed:

1. In His divinity Christ was anointed by God in eternity to be the Messiah—Christ—the anointed One (Dan. 9:26; John 1:41).

2. Christ came in His incarnation as the anointed One to accomplish God's eternal plan (Luke 2:11; Matt. 1:16; 16:16).

3. In His humanity Christ was anointed again in time at His baptism for His ministry, mainly on the earth (3:16-17; Luke 4:18-19; Heb. 1:9; Acts 10:38).

4. In His resurrection Christ became the life-giving Spirit for the purpose of being God's Anointed, and in His ascension He was made both Lord and Christ, becoming God's Anointed in an official way to carry out God's commission, mainly in His heavenly ministry (1 Cor. 15:45b; Acts 2:36).

Day 3   C. Psalm 2:4-6 is God's declaration concerning Christ:

1. In His ascension Christ was installed as God's King for God's kingdom (v. 6; Acts 5:31; Rev. 1:5a).

2. God proclaimed that He had installed Christ upon Mount Zion, not upon Mount Sinai (Heb. 12:18-22; Gal. 4:25-26):

a. Mount Sinai was the place where the law was given; Mount Zion in the heavens is the place where Christ is today in His ascension (Rev. 14:1; Psa. 68:15-16; Eph. 4:8).

    b. The New Testament believers have come
not to Mount Sinai but to Mount Zion,
where we have the church, the Body of
Christ, and God's economy for God's testimony (Heb. 12:18-24).

    c. Mount Sinai produces children of slavery
under the law, but our mother, the Jerusalem above, which is in the heavens at
Mount Zion, produces children of promise
who inherit the promised blessing—the
all-inclusive Spirit (Gal. 4:24-26, 28; 3:14).

Day 4 D. Psalm 2:7-9 is the declaration of Christ Himself:

    1. Verse 7 is quoted by the apostle Paul in Acts
13:33, indicating that Psalm 2:7 refers to
Christ's resurrection.

    2. After being cut off, crucified (Dan. 9:26), Christ,
God's anointed One, was resurrected to be
begotten in His humanity as the firstborn
Son of God (Psa. 2:7; Acts 13:33; Rom. 1:3-4;
8:29; Heb. 1:5-6):

    a. *Today* in Psalm 2:7 is the day of Christ's
resurrection.

    b. By resurrection Christ brought His human-
ity into the divine sonship and was designated the Son of God with His humanity;
His resurrection was His birth as God's firstborn Son (Rom. 1:3-4; 8:29; Acts 13:33):

    1) Before His incarnation Christ already
was the Son of God, the only begotten
Son (John 1:18; Rom. 8:3).

    2) By incarnation Christ put on an ele-
ment, the human flesh, which had
nothing to do with divinity; that part
of Him needed to be sanctified and uplifted by passing through death and
resurrection (John 1:14; Rom. 1:3-4).

    3) By resurrection His human nature
was sanctified, uplifted, and transformed; hence, by resurrection He was
designated the Son of God with His

humanity, and now, as the Son of God, He possesses humanity as well as divinity (Acts 13:33; Heb. 1:5).

4) God is using such a Christ, the first-born Son, as the producer and as the prototype, the model, to produce His many sons (Rom. 8:29).

c. Through the same resurrection all His believers were born with Him to be His many brothers, the many sons of God (John 20:17; 1 Pet. 1:3; Rom. 8:29; Heb. 2:10).

Day 5   3. Christ has been given the nations as His inheritance and the limits of the earth as His possession (Psa. 2:8; 72:8, 11; Rev. 11:15).

4. Christ will rule the nations in His kingdom with an iron rod (Psa. 2:9; Rev. 2:26-27; 19:15).

E. Psalm 2:10-12 is the preaching of the gospel:

1. These verses are a warning concerning the coming wrath of God and Christ upon the world:

a. One day Christ will come to execute His judgment in His wrath (v. 12; Rev. 6:15-17; Joel 1:15; 2:11, 31; 3:14; 1 Cor. 4:3-5).

b. In the New Testament the period in which Christ will come to execute His judgment in His wrath upon the world is called "the day of the Lord" (Acts 2:20; 1 Cor. 5:5; 1 Thes. 5:2; 2 Thes. 2:2; 2 Pet. 3:10), which is also the day of God (v. 12; Joel 1:15).

Day 6   2. We all need to realize that we are nothing and vanity (Psa. 39:4-5); our realizing that we are nothing, that our condition is sinful, and that our situation is one of vanity opens the way for Christ to crucify us and enter into us to replace us by living Himself through us and causing us to live together with Him in an organic union (Gal. 2:20).

3. To take refuge in the Son is to believe into the Son, Christ, taking Him as our refuge, protection, and hiding place, and to kiss the Son is

to love the Son and thereby to enjoy Him
(Psa. 2:12; John 3:16, 36):

a. To believe in the Lord is to receive Him,
and to love the Lord is to enjoy Him (1 Tim.
1:14).

b. The Gospel of John presents faith and love
as the two requirements for us to participate in the Lord (3:16; 14:23).

c. Through faith we receive the Lord, and
through love we enjoy the Lord whom we
have received (1:12; 14:21, 23; 21:15-17;
Eph. 6:23).

Morning Nourishment

Col. Who is the image of the invisible God, the Firstborn of
1:15 all creation.
18-19 And He is the Head of the Body, the church; He is the
      beginning, the Firstborn from the dead, that He Him-
      self might have the first place in all things; for in Him
      all the fullness was pleased to dwell.

The spirit of the Bible is just to exalt Christ. When we come to
study the Psalms, we must realize this. We must realize that we
cannot exalt anything higher than Christ. If we exalt anyone or
anything other than Christ, we break the spirit of the Bible. If we
are going to interpret any types or explain any parables, we must
take care of this spirit. The spirit of the Bible is to exalt Christ.

The spirit of the Bible exalts the Christ ordained by God to have
the preeminence (the first place) in the old creation, in the new creation, in the Body of Christ, and in everything (Col. 1:15-19). Also
the spirit of the Bible does not give any orthodox position to the law
(Gal. 4:21-25) given by God alongside His economy (Rom. 5:20a).

Many teachings...today are off the mark because they do not
take care of the lines, the principles, and the spirit of the Bible....A
prophet is one who has received the word from God. Then he
speaks the word in the line of the tree of life, in the proper principles, and in the spirit of exalting Christ. In whatever we speak, we
must have a spirit to exalt Christ. (*Life-study of the Psalms,* p. 112)

Today's Reading

Colossians 1:15-19 shows that the spirit of the Bible exalts
Christ. These five verses are unique in the Bible in exalting Christ.
Christ must have the first place; He must have the preeminence.

Since He has the first place in all things, we must give Him the
first place in our being and in all that we do. He must be first in
our marriage, in our spending of money, and in our demeanor. In
the way that we dress, we must give Christ the preeminence.

Whenever we study a book of the Bible, we must keep the lines,
the principles, and the spirit of the Bible. Then the light comes. If
we read the Bible without seeing the lines, the principles, and the

spirit of the Bible, we will not know what it is talking about.

The Bible does not exalt the law or the prophets. The spirit of the Bible exalts only one person—Christ.

We must understand why Psalms 1 and 2 were sovereignly arranged in this way. Psalm 1 is concerning the keeping of the law. Immediately after Psalm 1, Christ is in Psalm 2 as the exalted One. The spirit of the Bible, from Genesis 1 through Revelation 22, reveals only Christ as the prominent One, as the first One, as God's centrality and universality. Eventually, the Bible concludes with a new city. The new city, the New Jerusalem, will be a complement of Christ and a complement to Christ. The spirit of the Bible does not exalt anything or anyone other than Christ.

Paul, in his fourteen Epistles, fought a battle to put down everything other than Christ. In his Epistle to the Galatians, Paul put down the law, circumcision, tradition, and religion. To him all things other than Christ were refuse (Phil. 3:8). He exalted only Christ.

Psalm 1 is according to the human concept of uplifting and treasuring the law, whereas Psalm 2 is according to the divine concept of exalting Christ as God's central stress.

Psalm 2 is a declaration of God according to His divine concept. ...[It] exalts Christ as the center of the economy of God. Although the word *economy* is not in Psalm 2, the revelation and reality of God's economy are there. In this psalm God declared that He had installed His King (v. 6). For God to have a King is for the fulfilling of His economy. Then God said, "I will give the nations as Your inheritance / And the limits of the earth as Your possession" (v. 8). This is for a kingdom. Of course, the King needs a kingdom, and this kingdom is not small. It is a great kingdom....This will be the biggest kingdom in human history. Christ will possess all the continents. His kingdom will be everywhere to include everyone. The King and the kingdom in Psalm 2 show us the economy of God. (*Life-study of the Psalms,* pp. 111-112, 29, 27, 32-33)

Further Reading: Life-study of the Psalms, msg. 8; *Life-study of Colossians,* msgs. 5, 8-10

Enlightenment and inspiration: _____

_____

_____

_____

Morning Nourishment

Psa. The kings of the earth take their stand, and the rulers
2:2, 4 sit in counsel together, against Jehovah and against
His Anointed:...He who sits in the heavens laughs;
the Lord has them in derision.

Eventually, Christ will rule the nations in His kingdom with
an iron rod (Psa. 2:9; Rev. 2:26-27). There is a marvelous sequence
in Psalm 2 revealing the steps of Christ in God's economy beginning from His being anointed in eternity in His divinity. We may
wonder where Christ's death is spoken of in Psalm 2, but we need
to realize that Christ's resurrection implies His death....Thus,
in Psalm 2 we see His being anointed in His divinity and humanity, His death, His resurrection, and His ascension with His
enthronement. God installed Him as King, enthroning Him to
give Him all the nations with the limits of the earth. This is to set
up a universal kingdom for Christ. Then Christ will rule the
nations with an iron rod. (*Life-study of the Psalms*, p. 36)

Today's Reading

We need to see the revelation concerning Christ in God's economy versus the law in man's appreciation in the Psalms....Now
we need to see the divine revelation of Christ in God's economy in
Psalm 2 (vv. 2, 6-9, 12).

Psalm 2 says that Christ is opposed by the rulers of the world.
Verses 1-3 say, "Why are the nations in an uproar, / And why do
the peoples contemplate a vain thing? / The kings of the earth
take their stand, / And the rulers sit in counsel together, / Against
Jehovah and against His Anointed: / Let us break apart their
bonds / And cast their ropes away from us." Soon after Christ's
ascension, on the earth at Peter's time, Herod and Pilate took
their stand against Christ. Acts 4:25-29a records the prayer of the
early church, in which they quote from Psalm 2. Acts 4:27 says,
"For truly in this city there were gathered together against Your
holy Servant Jesus, whom You anointed, both Herod and Pontius
Pilate, with the Gentiles and the peoples of Israel." They all were
opposing Christ. (*Life-study of the Psalms*, pp. 32, 36-37)

In Revelation 13 we saw two beasts—Antichrist and the false prophet, both of whom collaborate with the dragon, Satan, to oppose God and to hinder the completion of God's economy.

Christ's enemies will become all the more evil, even declaring war against Him. Therefore, Christ, the Bridegroom, will come with His bride to fight against them.

God has prepared the lake of fire as a "trash can" to dispose of all the trash in the universe. Antichrist, the false prophet, and their armies will be swept into the "dust pan" and then dumped into the lake of fire. After the millennium, Satan himself will join them there. After the judgment at the great white throne, all the dead unbelievers will also be cast into the lake of fire. From that time onward, there will be no more dust. In the New Jerusalem, there will be no dust; there will be only gold, pearl, and precious stones. The Lord's fighting in the war at Armageddon will actually be a sweeping of dirt into the universal "trash can." The Lord may say to Antichrist, "…Have you declared war on Me? This gives Me the perfect opportunity to sweep you away. My bride will cooperate with me in doing this." (*Life-study of Revelation*, pp. 527, 634-635)

Both *Messiah* (from Hebrew) and *Christ* (from Greek) mean *the anointed One* [Psa. 2:2]. In His divinity Christ was anointed by God in eternity to be the Messiah—Christ—the anointed One (Dan. 9:26; John 1:41). He came in His incarnation as the anointed One to accomplish God's eternal plan (Luke 2:11; Matt. 1:16; 16:16). In His humanity He was anointed again in time at His baptism for His ministry, mainly on the earth (Matt. 3:16-17; Luke 4:18-19; Acts 10:38; Heb. 1:9). In His resurrection Christ became the life-giving Spirit (1 Cor. 15:45) for the purpose of being God's Anointed, and in His ascension He was made both Lord and Christ (Acts 2:36), becoming God's Anointed in an official way to carry out God's commission, mainly in His heavenly ministry. See footnote 1 on John 1:41 and footnote 1 on Acts 2:36. (Psa. 2:2, footnote 1)

Further Reading: Christ and the Church Revealed and Typified in the Psalms, chs. 1-2; Life-study of Revelation, msg. 55

Enlightenment and inspiration: _____

_____

_____

_____

Morning Nourishment

Psa. But I have installed My King upon Zion, My holy
2:6   mountain.
Heb. But you have come forward to Mount Zion and to
12:22 the city of the living God, the heavenly Jerusalem;
       and to myriads of angels, to the universal gathering.

The twelve verses of Psalm 2 can be divided into four sections, with three verses in each section. The first three verses predict the opposition of the world rulers to Christ. This prophecy began to be fulfilled at the time Christ was judged by Pilate. Its fulfillment will be continued until the time indicated in Revelation 19:19. At the time Jesus was betrayed, the rulers, the kings, the judges of this earth, began to oppose Him. So this psalm says, "Why are the nations in an uproar, / And why do the peoples contemplate a vain thing? / The kings of the earth take their stand, / And the rulers sit in counsel together, / Against Jehovah and against His Anointed" (vv. 1-3). This includes…the opposition of world leaders to Christ from the time of His crucifixion till the time the Antichrist will be defeated by Christ. (*Christ and the Church Revealed and Typified in the Psalms*, p. 16)

Today's Reading

The second section of Psalm 2 is God's declaration (vv. 4-6). Verse 4 says, "He who sits in the heavens laughs."…While the… world rulers were plotting against Christ, God undoubtedly was in the heavens laughing at them and having them in derision.… Where are the Roman Caesars [today]? Where will today's Christ-opposing rulers be a few years from now? God is laughing and saying, "What are you doing? Your opposition can only last a few fleeting years." The judges and kings arise and fight against Christ, but eventually God will destroy them. "Then He will speak to them in His anger, / And in His burning wrath He will terrify them" (v. 5). God said, "I have installed My King / Upon Zion, My holy mountain" (v. 6). This is the declaration of God. (*Christ and the Church Revealed and Typified in the Psalms*, pp. 16-17)

The first psalm is concerning keeping the law, and the second psalm tells us to kiss Christ. Which is higher? I am not asking which one is right or wrong, but which one is higher. Surely, kissing the Son is higher than keeping the law.

We secretly, unconsciously, and subconsciously hold our natural concept in coming to the Bible. This is why we do not receive the revelation from the Bible into us. Instead, we insert our concept into the Bible. We should not exalt the keeping of the law, because the book of Psalms itself does not go along with this. If we are exalting the keeping of the law in Psalm 1, we are then confronted with Psalm 2. Psalm 2 is God's speaking, God's declaration, concerning Christ as the center of His economy. He declares, "I have installed My King / Upon Zion, My holy mountain" (v. 6). This is not ordinary speaking, but a declaration and a proclamation.

God proclaimed to all His people that He had installed His King upon Mount Zion, not Mount Sinai. These two mountains—Mount Zion and Mount Sinai—are very significant. Hebrews 12 says that we have not come to Mount Sinai but to Mount Zion (vv. 18-22). Mount Sinai was the place where the law was given, and Mount Zion is the place where Christ is today in the heavens in His ascension.

Paul speaks of these mountains in Galatians 4. Mount Sinai produces children of slavery, but our mother, the Jerusalem above, is in the heavens, at Mount Zion (vv. 25-26). Revelation 14:1 tells us that there are a hundred and forty-four thousand standing with the Lamb on Mount Zion. These hundred and forty-four thousand are not praising God for the law given at Mount Sinai. Mount Zion is not a place to show us the law, the commandments. It is a place to show us Christ—only Christ. Mount Sinai is in the Bible, but the spirit of the Bible does not exalt it. Instead, the Bible puts Mount Sinai down to a lower place. The spirit of the Bible exalts only Christ. (*Life-study of the Psalms,* pp. 30-31)

Further Reading: Life-study of Galatians, msg. 24; *Life-study of Hebrews,* msg. 53

Enlightenment and inspiration: _____

_____

_____

_____

Morning Nourishment

Psa. **I will recount the decree of Jehovah; He said to Me:**
2:7-9 **You are My Son; today I have begotten You. Ask of Me,**
and I will give the nations as Your inheritance and
the limits of the earth as Your possession. You will
break them with an iron rod; You will shatter them
like a potter's vessel.

The third section [of Psalm 2], verses 7 through 9, is the declaration of Christ Himself. Christ declared something. He said, "I
will recount the decree of Jehovah; / He said to Me: You are My
Son; / Today I have begotten You." Both Acts 13 and Hebrews 1
tell us that this word refers to the resurrection of Christ. Christ
was begotten as the Son of God by being resurrected. Then He
ascended to the heavens, where He asked of the Father, and the
Father gave Him all the nations as His inheritance. God granted
to Him the uttermost parts of the earth for His possession, and
God said, "You will break them with an iron rod; / You will shatter
them like a potter's vessel." (*Christ and the Church Revealed and
Typified in the Psalms,* p. 17)

Today's Reading

After passing through thirty-three and a half years of human
living, Christ was cut off (Dan. 9:26). That means He was crucified.

After being cut off, crucified, Christ was resurrected to be begotten as the firstborn Son of God (Psa. 2:7; Acts 13:33; Heb. 1:5-6).
Psalm 2 shows us Christ's resurrection. The word *resurrection* is
not there, but the fact is there. Verse 7 says, "I will recount the
decree of Jehovah; / He said to Me: You are My Son; / Today I have
begotten You." "Today" is the day of Christ's resurrection. In Acts
13:33 Paul quoted Psalm 2:7, telling us that this refers to Christ's
resurrection. In His resurrection, Christ was begotten. Since He
was already the Son of God, why did He need to be begotten as the
Son of God in resurrection? Christ was the only begotten Son of
God in His divinity (John 3:16), but when He became incarnated,
He put humanity upon Him. This humanity had nothing to do

with the sonship of God, but through His death and resurrection, His humanity was "sonized" to also be the Son of God. By resurrection Christ brought His humanity into the divine sonship and was designated the Son of God with His humanity (Rom. 1:4). Now the Son of God has the divine nature with the human nature. When Christ was merely the only begotten Son of God, He was God's Son only in the divine nature. Now as the firstborn Son of God, He possesses both the divine nature and the human nature.

Christ is the firstborn Son of God, and we are the many sons of God. We believers in Christ are regenerated sons of God, having God's life and God's nature, but we also have our human nature. Our human nature is still in the process of being begotten. We have been regenerated in our spirit, but we still have not been transfigured in our body. When our body is transfigured, redeemed, glorified, our body will also be "sonized." Our sonship will be completed by that time (Rom. 8:23). The sonship began with the regeneration of our spirit, is continuing with the transformation of our soul, and will be consummated with the redemption of our body. The process of our sonship passes through our regeneration and transformation to our glorification.

In Psalm 2 we can see God's economy with God's kingdom and the resurrection of Christ, in which He was begotten to be God's firstborn Son. The day of resurrection was a great day. Not only was Christ born on that day, but we also were born on that day. First Peter 1:3 says that through Christ's resurrection, God regenerated us. When Christ was born as the firstborn Son of God, we were all born with Him to be His many brothers, the many sons of God (Rom. 8:29). Christ's resurrection was a big delivery, a big birth, of Himself as the firstborn Son of God with His many brothers, the many sons of God. (*Life-study of the Psalms,* pp. 34-35)

Further Reading: Life-study of Acts, msg. 37; *Life-study of 1 Peter,* msg. 3

Enlightenment and inspiration: _____

_____

_____

_____

Morning Nourishment

Psa. Now therefore, O kings, be prudent; take the admoni-
2:10-12 tion, O judges of the earth. Serve Jehovah with fear,
and rejoice with trembling. Kiss the Son lest He be
angry and you perish from the way; for His anger
may suddenly be kindled. Blessed are all those who
take refuge in Him.

According to Psalm 2:8, Christ has been given the nations as
His inheritance and the limits of the earth as His possession for His
kingdom. When the Lord came back to the disciples in His resurrection, He told them, "All authority has been given to Me in heaven
and on earth" (Matt. 28:18). The Lord's word here covers what is
mentioned in Psalm 2:8. God has given all the nations on this earth
to Christ as His inheritance. Furthermore, God has given the limits of the earth to Christ as His possession. Today if you own even a
small portion of land in Taiwan, you are a rich man. But the entire
earth will be possessed by Christ. This is His land. How rich He is!
We cannot see such wonderful things about Christ in Psalm 1.
Psalm 1 says, according to the human concept, that the man who
meditates in the law will prosper in everything, but Psalm 2
reveals, according to the divine concept, that God has given the
limits of the earth to Christ. (*Life-study of the Psalms*, pp. 35-36)

Today's Reading

The last section [of Psalm 2], verses 10 to 12, is the gospel
preaching. "Now therefore, O kings, be prudent; / Take the
admonition, O judges of the earth. / Serve Jehovah with fear, /
And rejoice with trembling." This simply means to repent and
believe. "Kiss the Son / Lest He be angry and you perish from
the way; /…Blessed are all those who take refuge in Him." The
last three verses of Psalm 2 are the gospel. (*Christ and the
Church Revealed and Typified in the Psalms*, p. 17)

Psalm 2 also gives a warning to the world (vv. 10-12)….
First, God and His Christ will be in wrath to the world (v. 12b;
Rev. 6:15-17). Men should not think that there is no God in
this universe or that Christ is just a name in religion. The

Bible tells us clearly that Christ is waiting for the opportunity to come to execute His judgment in His anger, in His wrath.

The book of Joel speaks of this judgment. The subject of Joel is the day of the Lord (1:15; 2:11, 31; 3:14), but few Christians understand what the day of the Lord is. Paul gave us the definition in 1 Corinthians 4:3-5. In verse 3 he said, "It is a very small thing that I should be examined by you or by man's day." Before the Lord comes, it is man's day, in which man judges. Today is man's day. In man's day, everything is judged by man. But after man's day, there will be a day which will be called the day of the Lord. This day will last about one thousand three and a half years. The day on which the great tribulation begins will be the beginning of the day of the Lord. From that day, the Lord's wrath will be expressed. The day of the Lord is the day of His judgment.

It may seem today that the Lord does not care for the world situation....But when the great tribulation begins, that will be the beginning of the day of the Lord. Christ will come to interfere with the world situation.

Joel reveals that after the three and a half years of the great tribulation, the Lord will judge the living Gentiles (3:12). Matthew 25 tells us that He will separate them, the sheep from the goats, in His judgment (vv. 32-46). Afterward, He will set up the thousand-year kingdom. In the thousand-year kingdom, He will judge, rule, and control the entire earth. At the end of that thousand years, there will be a rebellion, which He will also judge (Rev. 20:8-9). Then He will have the final judgment on the great white throne to judge the dead unbelievers (vv. 11-15). That will be the end of the day of the Lord.

Since God and His Christ will be in wrath to the world, man must repent (Psa. 2:11; Acts 17:30). This is the New Testament gospel. (*Life-study of the Psalms,* pp. 37-38)

Further Reading: Life-study of Joel, msgs. 1-3; *Life-study of Matthew,* msg. 67

Enlightenment and inspiration: _____

_____

_____

_____

Morning Nourishment

Psa.   O Jehovah, cause me to know my end, and the mea-
39:4-5 sure of my days, what it is. May I know how transient
       I am. Behold, You have made my days as *mere* hand-
       breadths, and my lifetime is as nothing before You;
       surely every man at his best is altogether vanity. Selah
Eph.   Peace to the brothers and love with faith from God
6:23   the Father and the Lord Jesus Christ.

The day of the Lord will last one thousand three and a half
years. After this day, the heavens and the earth will be burned to
become the new heavens and new earth. Then the New Jerusalem
will come in, and righteousness will fill the new heavens and new
earth (2 Pet. 3:13). Everything will be right. There will be no more
need for any kind of judgment. (*Life-study of the Psalms,* p. 38)

Today's Reading

David realized the nothingness and vanity of his life and
asked God to remove His chastening (for his transgressions) from
him and look away from him as a stranger and sojourner (Psa.
39:4-13). We always think that we are something and somebody,
but David was brought by the Lord into a situation to realize that
actually he was nothing and vanity. David said that every man at
his best is altogether vanity (v. 5)....We need to realize that our
condition is sinful, and our situation is one of vanity.

The Bible tells us that the word of the Lord is the truth, the
reality (John 17:17), and also the light (Psa. 119:105). Through
the truth and light released in these messages, I hope that we can
see what God wants us to be. God wants us to be nothing. God
wants us to be replaced by Christ. Therefore, what God wants was
expressed by Paul when he said, "I am crucified with Christ; and
it is no longer I who live, but it is Christ who lives in me" (Gal.
2:20a). Christ has crucified me, and Christ has come into me to
replace me. Now I have an organic union with Him. He lives and
works, and I live and work with Him. Christ replaces me to live
Himself through me. This is the divine concept of God according
to the divine revelation of the New Testament.

Psalm 2:12b says, "Blessed are all those who take refuge in Him." To take refuge in the Son equals to believe into the Son, Christ (John 3:16)....We can see this with the type of Noah's ark. When all the people trusted, or believed in, that ark, they all entered into that ark, to take the ark as their refuge, protection, and hiding place. Today our Christ is our refuge, our protection. We are hiding ourselves in Him.

Psalm 2:12a says that we need to kiss the Son. The New Testament tells us that we need faith and love:..."The grace of our Lord superabounded with faith and love in Christ Jesus" [1 Tim. 1:14]. The Lord's grace visited Paul and superabounded in him with faith and love in Christ. One day he received mercy and grace from the Lord, not only to believe in Him but also to love Him. We have been given faith to believe into Christ, taking Him as our refuge. Also, we have been given God's love to love the Lord Jesus.

In the Gospel of John, we are taught that we need to believe into Christ, the Son (1:12), and to love Him (14:23). In the last chapter of John, chapter twenty-one, the very Christ who is our refuge came back to Peter to restore Peter's love toward Him. The Lord asked Peter three times, "Do you love Me?" (vv. 15-17).

A young believer may be strong to boldly tell the Lord that he loves Him and will never deny Him. But when he is defeated, his natural confidence in his love toward the Lord will be dealt with. Then he will learn to follow the Lord and to love the Lord without any confidence in his natural strength.

To believe in the Lord is to receive Him; to love the Lord is to enjoy Him. The Gospel of John presents these as the two requirements for us to participate in the Lord. The Lord is within us to be our faith and to be our love. To love Him, according to Psalm 2:12a, is to kiss Him. We should not uplift and treasure the law. Instead, we should kiss Christ, love Christ, day by day. (*Life-study of the Psalms,* pp. 218-219, 38-39)

Further Reading: Life-study of the Psalms, msgs. 3, 17; *The Conclusion of the New Testament,* msg. 345

Enlightenment and inspiration: _____

_____

_____

_____

Hymns, #1094

1 Lo, the nations all assemble
      And imagine vanity,
   Kings and princes plot together
      'Gainst the Lord in unity.
   "Let us break their bonds asunder,
      Cast away their cords from us."
   'Gainst the Lord and His Anointed
      Worldly rulers counsel thus.

2 He who sitteth in the heavens
      In contempt will laugh at them,
   Vex them in His fierce displeasure,
      Terrifying all such men.
   Yet upon the hill of Zion
      God has His anointed King—
   This is God's own declaration,
      All the kings admonishing.

3 Now 'tis Christ, 'tis God's Anointed,
      Who declares the Lord's decree:
   "Thou'rt my Son (in resurrection),
      This day I've begotten Thee.
   All the nations I will give Thee
      For Thine own inheritance.
   Thou shalt dash them into pieces
      In Thy kingly excellence."

4 Now be wise, O be instructed,
      All ye rulers of the earth,
   Fear the Lord, rejoice with trembling,
      Serve the only One of worth.
   Kiss the Son, lest He be angry
      And ye perish in the way.
   "All who trust in Him are blessed,"
      All who trust in Him will say.

5 Lord, we praise Thee, we have seen Him—
      Thy unique Anointed One—
   And from vanity repenting,
      We in love have kissed Thy Son.
   "All who trust in Him are blessed"—
      Not "all those who keep the law."
   In that risen One believing,
      We are blest forevermore.

Composition for prophecy with main point and sub-points: _____

_____

_____

_____

_____

_____

_____

_____

_____

_____

_____

_____

_____

_____

_____

_____

_____

_____

_____

_____

_____

_____

_____

_____

_____

_____

_____

_____

_____

_____

_____

_____

_____

_____

_____

The Excellency of Christ

Scripture Reading: Psa. 8

Day 1   I. **Psalm 8 shows that God's purpose and plan for man to express Him with His image and to represent Him with His dominion have never changed (Gen. 1:26):**
   A. The man prophesied in Psalm 8 is the second man, the Lord Jesus, who has recovered man's lost ordination and has fulfilled God's original purpose (Heb. 2:5-9).
   B. This second man is also a corporate man, the new man, the corporate Christ, who expresses God in His image and represents God to have dominion over all things for the fulfillment of God's purpose (Eph. 2:15; Col. 3:10-11; Acts 9:4-5; Eph. 1:22-23; Heb. 2:10-11).

   II. **Psalm 8 is David's inspired praise of the excellency of Christ—this psalm speaks of the heavens, the earth, babes and sucklings, man, three categories of enemies, and the Lord's incarnation, human living, death, resurrection, and ascension, the Body of Christ, His coming back, and His kingdom.**

   III. **The Lord's name is excellent (majestic) in all the earth, and His splendor (glory) has been set over the heavens (v. 1):**
   A. In Psalms 3 through 7 it was a mess on the earth, according to David's human concept.
   B. Here in Psalm 8 the name of the incarnated, crucified, resurrected, ascended, and exalted Jesus (Phil. 2:5-11) is excellent (majestic) in all the earth according to the divine revelation, and the Lord's glory is over the heavens in the sight of David.
   C. The goal of this psalm is to join the earth to the heavens and bring the heavens down to the earth, making the earth and the heavens one (John 1:51; Gen. 28:12).

Day 2   **IV. Out of the mouths of babes and sucklings the Lord has established strength (praise—Matt. 21:16) because of His adversaries, to stop the enemy and the avenger (Psa. 8:2):**

A. Babes and sucklings are the youngest, smallest, and weakest among men, indicating the highest consummation of the Lord's work in His redemption.

B. The Lord has established praise out of the mouths of babes and sucklings because of His adversaries (within) and for the stopping of the enemy and the avenger (without).

C. Satan is God's adversary within God's kingdom, God's enemy outside God's kingdom, and the avenger who roves to and fro over the earth (cf. Job 1:7; 1 Pet. 5:8).

Day 3   **V. David saw the heavens, the works of the Lord's fingers, the moon and the stars, which the Lord has ordained (Psa. 8:3):**

A. The moon and the stars indicate that David had this view—a view turned from looking at the earth to contemplating the heavens in the night.

B. In this view David had a pure vision to see the pure work in God's creation and ordination.

C. The aim in the Lord's redemption is to turn us from the messy earth to the bright heaven.

VI. What is mortal man, that the Lord remembers him, and the son of man, that He visits him? (v. 4):

A. In his view in the heavens, David turned his consideration to man on the earth.

B. Man is the central object of God in His creation for the accomplishment of His economy to fulfill His heart's desire.

C. The first "man" in verse 4 is *enosh* in Hebrew, and the second "man" is *adam* in Hebrew, both referring to:

1. The God-created man in God's creation in Genesis 1:26.

2. The Satan-captured man in man's fall in Psalm 8:4.

3. Christ as a man in His incarnation for the accomplishment of God's redemption in Hebrews 2:6.

D. Such a man God remembers in His economy and visits in His incarnation (John 1:14; Phil. 2:7).

Day 4 **VII. The Lord has made man a little lower than angels (Psa. 8:5a; Heb. 2:7a):**

A. This refers to Christ's incarnation with His human living for His all-inclusive death (John 1:14; Heb. 2:9a).

B. In His incarnation Christ was made a little lower than angels, physically not positionally, in the sense of being in the flesh.

VIII. God has crowned man (Christ) with glory and honor (Psa. 8:5b; Heb. 2:7b):

A. This refers to Christ's resurrection in His glory (John 7:39b; Luke 24:26) and His ascension in His honor (Acts 2:33-36; 5:31a).

B. This was through His all-inclusive death (Heb. 2:9).

IX. Psalm 8:2-5 shows us how the babes and sucklings are produced:

A. In order to produce babes and sucklings, God has visited man (v. 4):

1. God visited man by becoming incarnated, by putting on humanity and becoming a man to be a little lower than the angels (v. 5a).

2. God visited man also by living on earth, dying, rising up from the dead, and ascending to the heavens to be crowned with glory and honor (v. 5b).

3. God visited man through the long journey of His process to become the life-giving Spirit to reach us and to enter into us (John 1:14; 1 Cor. 15:45b; 6:17; cf. 1 Pet. 2:12; Luke 1:68, 78).

4. The incarnated One has become the life-giving Spirit, and it is this One who produces babes and sucklings.

Day 5 B. We become babes and sucklings in the initial stage through regeneration:

1. We are remade, re-created, through regeneration (cf. Matt. 18:3; 19:14).
2. Regeneration reduces our natural activity.
3. The proper, genuine salvation stops our human doing and makes us babes and sucklings to praise the Lord.

C. The process of producing babes and sucklings continues with sanctification, renewing, and transformation (Heb. 2:11; Rom. 12:2; 2 Cor. 3:18).

D. The Lord has perfected praise, or established strength, out of the mouths of babes and sucklings for the purpose of stopping His adversaries, the enemy, and the avenger (Psa. 8:2):

1. God overcomes His enemy through babes and sucklings, the youngest, smallest, and weakest among men; this is the Lord's recovery and victory (cf. 1 Cor. 1:26-31).
2. All things will be ruled over by Christ with His Body, and all things will be subjected under His feet (Psa. 8:6-8).
3. The perfected praise of the babes and sucklings is the ultimate consummation of the Lord's work of incarnation, human living, death, resurrection, ascension, and coming back to rule on earth:
   a. We may praise the Lord, but our praise needs to be perfected; through transformation we are perfected in praising the Lord.
   b. The perfected praise is the praise for the Lord's incarnation, human living, death, resurrection, ascension, and kingdom.
   c. In order to praise the Lord, we need to see Jesus, turning our view from the messy earth to the bright heaven (Heb. 2:9; 12:1-2).
   d. The perfected praise is the strength out of the mouths of babes and sucklings, the praise that defeats the adversaries, the enemy, and the avenger (2 Chron. 20:22; cf. vv. 12, 20-21).

4. "Through Him then let us offer up a sacrifice of praise continually to God, that is, the fruit of lips confessing His name" (Heb. 13:15).

Day 6   **X. God has caused man (Christ) to rule over the works of God's hands and has put all things under His feet: all sheep and oxen, the beasts of the field, the birds of heaven, the fish of the sea, and whatever passes through the paths of the seas (Psa. 8:6-8; Heb. 2:7b-8a):**

A. This word was fulfilled in Adam (Gen. 1:26-28), but it was broken by man's fall.

B. In Christ's ascension God subjected all things under Christ's feet and gave Him to be Head over all things to the church, which is His Body (Eph. 1:22-23; Rom. 16:20):

1. In the Body life we participate in the transmission of Christ's subjecting power to put all things under the feet of His Body.

2. The God of peace crushes Satan under the feet of those who live the church life as the practical expression of the Body (v. 20).

C. This word will be fulfilled in full in the millennium, the age of restoration (Rev. 20:4-6; Matt. 19:28; Isa. 11:6-9; 65:25).

XI. O Jehovah our Lord, how excellent (majestic) is Your name in all the earth! (Psa. 8:9):

A. Verse 9 repeats the first part of verse 1 to strengthen the thought concerning the excellency of the Lord's name in all the earth.

B. This makes the earth as excellent as the heavens, as indicated in the first part of the Lord's prayer: "Our Father who is in the heavens, Your name be sanctified; Your kingdom come; Your will be done, as in heaven, so also on earth" (Matt. 6:9-10).

Good to praise the Lord for something specific, what we enjoy & experience of Christ. This is part of the perfected praise.

Morning Nourishment

Heb. ..."What is man, that You bring him to mind? Or the
2:6-9 son of man, that You care for him? You have made
Him a little inferior to the angels; You have crowned
Him with glory and honor and have set Him over the
works of Your hands; You have subjected all things
under His feet."...But now we do not yet see all things
subjected to Him, but we see Jesus, who was made a
little inferior to the angels because of the suffering of
death, crowned with glory and honor...

Hebrews 2 discloses that the man mentioned in Psalm 8 is Christ.
God made Christ a little lower than the angels—this was the incarnation, and He was a man by the name of Jesus. After the incarnation this man was crowned with glory and honor in His ascension,
including His resurrection. Christ was crowned with glory and
honor because He resurrected and ascended to the heavens.
Therefore, the ascension includes the resurrection. Then it says
that all things were put under His feet. This is His dominion over
all things. Now Christ has the dominion, the lordship, the headship, and the kingdom. Just this little word *feet* indicates His
Body. He has a Body. Ephesians 1:22 and 23 say that God "subjected all things under His feet and gave Him to be Head over all
things to the church, which is His Body." The two feet are parts of
the Body. Hence, we have the incarnation, the resurrection, the
ascension, the enthronement, the lordship, the kingship, the
kingdom, and the Body of Christ. The Body is the many saints
who will be brought into glory according to Hebrews 2. The day
will come when He will be the Head in God's dominion, and we
will be the Body under His lordship and in His kingdom to rule
over the whole earth. In that day we will all shout, "O Jehovah our
Lord, how excellent is Your name in all the earth!" Today we must
have foresight to see through to the end. We must not care for
today's situation; we must set our eyes upon that day. Sooner or
later that day will come. Sooner or later all these pitiful situations
will be past. Praise the Lord! (*Christ and the Church Revealed
and Typified in the Psalms,* pp. 29-30)

Today's Reading

Psalm 2 tells us that Christ is the center of God's administration in the entire universe. Then Psalm 8 continues by telling us that this Christ is the incarnated and resurrected One, the One who has ascended to the heavens and is enthroned and crowned with glory and honor. He has the lordship, the headship, the kingship, and the dominion over all things with His Body. He is a marvelous Christ! If we have seen this Christ, we can do nothing but praise Him.

In Psalms 3 through 7 the writers were occupied with the adversaries and their own problems, so they asked God to solve these problems. But the answer is in Psalm 8. It is by Christ incarnated, identified with man, crowned with glory, and made, with His Body, to have dominion over all things, that the problem on earth can be solved. The solution includes the incarnation up to the time of the kingdom; then when the kingdom comes, Christ with His Body will have dominion over all things. At that time all earth's problems will be solved. This is the content of Psalm 8. Why is the name of the Lord so excellent in all the earth? Because Christ was incarnated to accomplish redemption, He was resurrected to impart life to His Body, He was crowned with glory, and He was enthroned and made to have dominion over all things with His Body. The day will come when Christ with His Body will exercise His authority.

The human race has done its utmost to solve its problems, but the more problems they solve, the more they have. The fact is that no one can solve the problems. You just wait praisingly. Hallelujah, Christ will come back! He has been made the Head over all things to the church. With His Body He will have the dominion over all. At that time, everything will be solved. (*Christ and the Church Revealed and Typified in the Psalms,* p. 31)

Further Reading: Christ and the Church Revealed and Typified in the Psalms, ch. 2; *God's Plan and God's Rest*

Enlightenment and inspiration: _____

_____

_____

Morning Nourishment

Psa. Out of the mouths of babes and sucklings You have
8:2 established strength because of Your adversaries, to
stop the enemy and the avenger.

Matt. ...And Jesus said to them, Yes. Have you never read,
21:16 "Out of the mouth of infants and sucklings You have
perfected praise"?

Psalm 8:2 shows us three negative categories of persons: the
adversaries, the enemy, and the avenger....In this universe, there
are still many adversaries, enemies, and avengers. Adversaries are
those who are within, enemies are those who are without, and the
avengers are those who run back and forth (cf. Job 1:7). Satan can be
signified by these three categories. First, Satan was within God's
kingdom. Then Satan became an enemy without, outside the kingdom of God. He is also the avenger, running back and forth....In
between the heavens and the earth, there are the adversaries
within, the enemy without, and the avenger running back and forth.

What would God do about this? God does something in a consummate way. He establishes His praises out of the mouths of
babes and sucklings, the youngest, smallest, and weakest ones.
Babes are a little stronger than sucklings, and sucklings are
somewhat smaller than the babes, but both of them are in the cat-
egory of the smallest and weakest. (*Life-study of the Psalms*, p. 54)

Today's Reading

[Do] we consider ourselves as babes and sucklings?...The Lord
Jesus told people, "Truly I say to you, Unless you turn and become
like little children, you shall by no means enter into the kingdom
of the heavens" (Matt. 18:3). He also said, "Allow the little children
and do not prevent them from coming to Me, for of such is the
kingdom of the heavens" (19:14). The Lord stressed that to participate in the kingdom of the heavens, we must be like little children. All the people who are in the kingdom of the heavens are as
babes. A brother may be over sixty years old, but in God's kingdom, he is a suckling.

Psalm 8:2 says that the Lord has established strength out of the mouths of babes and sucklings. Seemingly, strength does not refer to something that comes out of the mouth. When the Lord quoted this verse in Matthew 21:16, He used the word *praise* instead of *strength*. Weaker ones in themselves cannot praise. To cry or weep does not require strength, but to praise requires strength. When we gossip, argue, or reason with people, that does not require strength. But without strength, we cannot praise the Lord. Some praises may come out of our mouth, but they cannot be considered as perfected praises, because they are not so full of strength. Praises should be full of strength. Many times when the saints are praising the Lord, we can see the strength.

To praise is to have the strength in our mouth. God can work in His redemption to such an extent that the weakest ones and the smallest ones can have the strength to praise Him. God has established this.

The Hebrew word for *established* is a hard word to translate. In the Lord's quotation in Matthew 21:16, it says that He has "perfected" praise out of the mouths of the babes and sucklings. Psalm 8 says that He established strength out of the mouths of babes and sucklings, but the Lord Jesus quoted it by saying that He perfected praise. Is our praise perfect? We have to admit that our praise is altogether imperfect. Psalm 8 is not a long psalm, but it is a completed, perfected, and perfect psalm. If we are short of strength, we cannot praise. If we do not have the extra strength, we cannot have a completed, perfected, and perfect praise.

On earth the Lord's name is excellent; above the heavens is the Lord's splendor, His glory. In between there are the adversaries, the enemy, and the avenger, who are stopped by the praise of strength that comes out of the mouths of the smallest ones and the weakest ones. This is God's marvelous consummation. The highest consummation of the Lord's work in His redemption is to perfect the praise to Him out of the mouths of the smallest and the weakest. (*Life-study of the Psalms,* pp. 54-56)

Further Reading: Praising

Enlightenment and inspiration: _____

_____

_____

_____

Morning Nourishment

Psa. When I see Your heavens, the works of Your fingers,
8:3-4 the moon and the stars, which You have ordained,
what is mortal man, that You remember him, and the
son of man, that You visit him?

Gen. And God said, Let Us make man in Our image,
1:26 according to Our likeness; and let them have dominion over the fish of the sea and over the birds of
heaven and over the cattle and over all the earth and
over every creeping thing that creeps upon the earth.

David saw the heavens, the works of the Lord's fingers, the
moon and the stars, which the Lord has ordained (Psa. 8:3). This
indicates that David had a view turned from looking at the earth
to contemplating the heavens, in the night. In the night, if you
look at the earth, you will see nothing because of the darkness.
But if you look up to contemplate the heavens, you will see the
moon and the stars. In this view David had a pure vision to see the
pure work in God's creation and ordination. In the universe there
is not only God's creation but also God's ordination. David saw the
divine order in the universe.

This is the aim in the Lord's redemption—to turn us from the
messy earth to the bright heaven. Before we were saved, we were
in a messy situation. But after we were saved...our view was
turned from looking at this messy earth to looking at the bright
heaven. When bad news comes to me, I have to exercise to turn my
view to look at the bright heaven. When I turn my view from the
bad news and look up to the heavens, I can praise. We must learn to
turn our view. The aim in the Lord's redemption is to turn our view
from the earth to the heavens. (*Life-study of the Psalms*, pp. 61-62)

Today's Reading

In Psalm 8:4 David asked, "What is mortal man, that You
remember him, / And the son of man, that You visit him?" In his
view in the heavens, David turned his consideration to man on
the earth. The ordination of the moon and the stars is marvelous.
Then how about man on this earth? We should not forget that the

psalmist in this psalm is trying the best to bring the heavens down and to bring the earth up to join with the heavens. He looked at the heavens with the moon and the stars. That is wonderful, but what about man? We may think that man is pitiful, but according to the divine view in this psalm, we are wrong. Man was pitiful in Adam and in the fallen situation, but today man in Christ is not pitiful. The man in Christ is wonderful.

Three portions of the Word speak of the same thing concerning man—Genesis 1, Psalm 8, and Hebrews 2. What is revealed in Psalm 8 was first spoken of in Genesis 1. Genesis 1 says that man was commissioned with the authority to rule over all the created things (vv. 26, 28). Psalm 8 repeats this. Then in Hebrews 2:6-8 Paul quotes Psalm 8. These three portions of the Word show us that man has been in three stages: created in Genesis 1, fallen in Psalm 8, and redeemed in Hebrews 2.

This redeemed man is no longer in a pitiful situation. He is joined to Jesus. Actually, Jesus, the incarnated God, first joined Himself with us. Now in His redemption we are joined to Him. There is an organic union between Him and us. Christ has passed through human living, and He died to solve our problems. Then He resurrected and ascended to be crowned and enthroned with glory and honor. He was breathed into us and poured out upon us. Today He is both in the heavens and also within us and outside of us....We are men who have been mingled with Christ.

Man is the central object of God in His creation for the accomplishment of His economy to fulfill His heart's desire....We should not forget Genesis 1, Psalm 8, and Hebrews 2. These three portions cover the three stages of man.

Such a man God remembers in His economy and visits in His incarnation (John 1:14; Phil. 2:7). Thank God for His remembrance, and thank God for His incarnation. He remembered us in His economy, and He visited us in His incarnation. (*Life-study of the Psalms*, pp. 62-63)

Further Reading: Life-study of the Psalms, msg. 5

Enlightenment and inspiration: _____

_____

_____

_____

Morning Nourishment

Psa. You have made Him a little lower than angels and
8:5-8 have crowned Him with glory and honor. For You
have caused Him to rule over the works of Your
hands; You have put all things under His feet: all
sheep and oxen, as well as the beasts of the field, the
birds of heaven and the fish of the sea, whatever
passes through the paths of the seas.

Psalm 8:5 says, "You have made Him a little lower than angels /
And have crowned Him with glory and honor."...Who is "Him" in
this verse? "Him" actually refers to the man Jesus. God has made
the man Jesus a little lower than the angels...(Psa. 8:5a; Heb.
2:7a). This refers to Christ's incarnation (John 1:14). In His incarnation Christ was made a little lower than angels in the sense of
being in the flesh. In the flesh Christ was lower than the angels.
(*Life-study of the Psalms*, pp. 58, 63)

Today's Reading

After His human living, He was resurrected, and in His resurrection, He was glorified. Then He ascended to the heavens, and
in His ascension, He was honored. "Crowned...with glory and
honor" indicates or implies two steps: Christ's resurrection and
His ascension. Before His resurrection and ascension, there was
the death of Christ. If there is no death, there is no resurrection,
and if there is no resurrection, there is no ascension. Furthermore, without His incarnation and human living, He was not
qualified to die. He had to become a man and live for thirty-three
and a half years. Thus, in Psalm 8:5 we can see all the steps of the
Triune God's process: incarnation, human living for thirty-three
and a half years, death, resurrection, and ascension.

God has crowned man (Christ) with glory and honor (Psa.
8:5b; Heb. 2:7b). This refers to Christ's resurrection in His glory.
Through resurrection He entered into glory; He was glorified in
His resurrection (John 7:39b; Luke 24:26). This also refers to
Christ's ascension in His honor (Acts 2:33-36; 5:31a). Christ's res-
urrection is mainly in His glory, and His ascension is mainly in

His honor. Glory refers to the condition. Honor refers to the position. Condition-wise, Christ is in glory. Position-wise, Christ is in honor. He has both glory in condition and honor in position.

This was through His all-inclusive death (Heb. 2:9). Without death He could have never entered into resurrection, and He could have never reached His ascension.

Psalm 8 has nine verses. Verse 1 and verses 6-9 are somewhat easy to understand. Verses 2-5, however, are very puzzling and not easy to understand. Why did the psalmist, after talking about the earth with the excellency of Jehovah's name and the heavens with the glory, turn to the babes and sucklings? We need to see that verses 2-5 show us how the babes and sucklings are produced.

Psalm 8 is all-inclusive. It talks about the earth, the heavens, man, and the coming kingdom. But in addition to the earth, the heavens, man, and the coming kingdom, there are the adversaries, the enemy, and the avenger. Verse 2 says that because of the Lord's adversaries, He has established strength, or perfected praise. The Lord has established strength or perfected praise out of the mouths of babes and sucklings for the purpose of stopping His adversaries, the enemy, and the avenger. In this way God kills "three birds with one stone." Because of the adversaries, the enemy, and the avenger, God makes the babes and sucklings to praise Him in a complete way.

Now we need to consider who the babes and sucklings are. The sucklings are even younger than the babes, the infants, because they are still feeding on their mother's milk. They are the youngest. The little babes and sucklings do not do anything. But after growing up, they do many things. To stop a person from doing things is nearly impossible, because all human beings are doers. The whole earth is filled with man's doings. Who can stop this? Only the Lord can. No unregenerated man is a babe or a suckling. We become babes and sucklings by regeneration. (*Life-study of the Psalms*, pp. 58, 63-66)

Further Reading: Life-study of the Psalms, msg. 5

Enlightenment and inspiration: _____

_____

_____

_____

Morning Nourishment

1 Cor. ...**The lowborn things of the world and the despised**
1:28-30 **things God has chosen, things which are not, that He**
might bring to nought the things which are, so that
no flesh may boast before God. But of Him you are in
Christ Jesus, who became wisdom to us from God: both
righteousness and sanctification and redemption.

We...have to realize that for the Lord to regenerate us, He had
to undergo a number of procedures, or processes. He had to become a man, to live on this earth, to die, to enter into Hades for
three days and three nights, and He had to rise up to become the
life-giving Spirit. As the Spirit, He comes into us to regenerate us.
Thus, regeneration comes out of all the procedures of the Lord.

He was also crowned with glory and honor (Psa. 8:5b). Glory refers
to His resurrection, implying His death. Without death He could not
have entered into resurrection. To be crowned with glory is to be glorified. To be crowned with honor implies the ascension. Therefore
in one verse, verse 5, we see Christ's incarnation, His all-inclusive
death implied, His resurrection for His glorification, and His ascension for Him to be honored. (*Life-study of the Psalms*, pp. 67-68)

Today's Reading

God visited man through the long journey of His process to
become the life-giving Spirit to reach us and to enter into us....
The incarnated One is now the life-giving Spirit. It is this One
that can produce the babes and the sucklings.

The babes and sucklings are produced through regeneration in
the initial stage. Then they continue to be produced in full through
their sanctification, renewing, and transformation. Through transformation they are perfected in praising the Lord. This is the
Lord's recovery and the Lord's victory. God overcomes His enemy
through these babes and sucklings. The work of Christianity is to
produce active ones; they endeavor to produce "giants." Our work
is to produce babes and sucklings.

Psalm 8:6-8 says, "You have caused Him to rule over the works
of Your hands; / You have put all things under His feet: / All sheep

and oxen, / As well as the beasts of the field, / The birds of heaven and the fish of the sea, / Whatever passes through the paths of the seas." These verses refer to the kingdom. All things will be ruled over by Christ with His Body, and all things will be subjected under His feet. This really perfects the praise, completes the praise, in this psalm. This short psalm reveals so much. It speaks of the heavens, the earth, babes and sucklings, man, three categories of enemies, and the Lord's incarnation, human living, death, resurrection, ascension, coming back, and kingdom.

We Christians may praise the Lord, but our praise needs to be perfected. We need to praise Him for His splendor above the heavens and His excellency on earth. Then we can praise Him for His incarnation for Him to come to visit us. Then we should go on to praise Him for His human living, for His death, for His resurrection, for His ascension, and for His kingdom. We have to praise Him with all these matters. Then our praises will be perfected, completed. This praise is the strength out of the mouths of babes and sucklings. Such perfected praise is the ultimate consummation of the Lord's work of incarnation, human living, death, resurrection, ascension, and coming back to rule on this earth.

When we come to the Lord's table, we stop every kind of human speaking and human doing. We stop our work. We are here at the table to do only one thing—to praise Him. In order to praise, we must stop our work. Thus, at the Lord's table, we all are the real babes and sucklings. While we are here being stopped from all of our doings to praise the Lord, the adversaries, the enemy, and the avenger are all defeated. This is a shame to God's enemy.

We need to remain in the condition and spirit of the Lord's table. Our Christian life should be like the Lord's table. When we go home after the Lord's table, we should continue to praise the Lord. We have to learn not to do too much.... [but] we should not be lazy. The point is that we should stop our human doings and be those who simply praise the Lord. (*Life-study of the Psalms,* pp. 68-69)

Further Reading: Life-study of the Psalms, msg. 5

Enlightenment and inspiration: _____

_____

_____

_____

Morning Nourishment

Psa. **O Jehovah our Lord, how excellent is Your name in**
8:9 **all the earth!**
Matt. **You then pray in this way: Our Father who is in the**
6:9-10 **heavens, Your name be sanctified; Your kingdom**
come; Your will be done, as in heaven, *so* also on earth.

God has caused man (Christ) to rule over the works of God's
hands and has put all things under His feet...(Psa. 8:6-8; Heb.
2:7b-8a). This word was fulfilled first in Adam (Gen. 1:26-28). But
this word was broken by man's fall. Today nothing is subject to us.
Even the mosquitoes still come to defeat us. Nothing today is
under us because the order has been fully destroyed by man's fall.
But there will be a time, the time of restoration, when everything
will be in a good order. This word will be fulfilled in full in Christ
in the millennium, the age of restoration (Rev. 20:4-6; Matt. 19:28).
Isaiah 11:6-9 and 65:25 speak of the wonderful divine order in the
time of restoration. This is because of Christ's redemption. (*Life-
study of the Psalms,* p. 64)

Today's Reading

Psalm 8 is a short psalm, but it comprises and implies Christ's
incarnation, human living, death, resurrection, ascension, and
His being crowned to be the Lord and Christ and the King of
kings, the unique Ruler of the entire universe. The day will come
when He will be in the kingdom for a thousand years to rule over
all the creatures. This is the revelation in Psalm 8.

The last verse of this psalm repeats the first part of the first
verse by saying, "O Jehovah our Lord, / How excellent is Your
name / In all the earth!" At the end of the psalm, David does not
say anything further about the heavens, because eventually the
earth will be as excellent as the heavens.

Psalm 8:9 repeats the first part of verse 1 by saying, "O Jehovah our Lord, / How excellent is Your name / In all the earth!" This
strengthens the thought concerning the excellency of the Lord's
name in all the earth. The earth now is full of the excellency of Christ.
Now the earth is not a messy earth but an excellent earth because

the excellency of the name of Christ fills all the earth. In this verse the psalmist considers that the earth is as excellent as the heavens, as indicated in the first part of the Lord's prayer: "Our Father who is in the heavens, Your name be sanctified; Your kingdom come; Your will be done, as in heaven, so also on earth" (Matt. 6:9-10).

I would like to repeat the goal of this psalm once more. The goal is to join the earth to the heavens and to bring down the heavens to the earth, making these two one. If we are victorious and overcoming every day, this is our reality. Today with us, the earth is joined to the heavens, the heavens are brought down to the earth, and the two are one. But with the unbelieving ones and with the defeated Christians, the heavens are far away and the earth is dark and messy. This is why the unbelievers need all kinds of worldly amusements and sinful pleasures. But we do not need them. We need only Christ and the church life.

When we live Christ and live in the church life, the heavens and the earth are one. With us, our earth is really joined to the heavens. With us, the heavens are always here. Here on earth we have the excellent name of Jesus. On this earth today the only excellency is with the name of Christ. Hallelujah! There is such a name! We have this precious name on earth, and we also have our splendor, our glory, above the heavens.

Eventually, with us, the earth and the heavens will be one in a complete way. In the coming age, in the millennium, in the age of restoration, the heaven is down and the earth is up. There we will enjoy God's salvation to the uttermost. In the millennium all of us will be babes and sucklings. There will be no older ones, no fatigued ones. Everyone will be fresh, young, living, and full of strength.

Today many Christians like power, but the Bible in Psalm 8 speaks of strength. We need to be full of strength to praise the Lord, to express God's consummated work in His redemption. (*Life-study of the Psalms,* pp. 58-59, 64-65)

Further Reading: Life-study of the Psalms, msg. 5

Enlightenment and inspiration: _____

_____

_____

_____

Hymns, #1097

1 O Lord, our Lord, how excellent
    Thy name in all the earth!
  Let every people, tribe, and tongue
    Proclaim its boundless worth.
  Out of the mouth of little ones
    Thou hast established praise,
  That Thou may still Thine enemy
    And swiftly end his days.

2 When we the universe behold,
    The work of Thy great hand—
  The sun, the moon, and all the stars
    By lofty wisdom planned;
  O what is man that Thou should'st care
    That Thou should'st mindful be?
  The son of man Thou visitest
    In Thine economy.

3 O Jesus Lord, Thou art that man,
    The One who joined our race,
  Who put upon Himself the flesh
    And took a lower place.
  But now with glory Thou art crowned,
    With sovereignty complete.
  Now through Thy Body Thou dost rule
    With all beneath Thy feet.

4 Thine incarnation, rising too,
    And Thy transcendency,
  Thy Lordship, Headship, kingdom full,
    And Body here we see.
  By all these steps of work divine
    Thou hast established praise.
  With overflowing hearts to Thee
    Our joyful voice we raise.

5 Oh, soon that blessed day shall come—
    All tongues these words shall peal!
  But in the local churches now
    We have a foretaste real.
  O Lord, our Lord, how excellent
    Thy name in all the earth!
  Let every people, tribe, and tongue
    Proclaim its boundless worth.

Composition for prophecy with main point and sub-points: _____

_____
_____
_____
_____
_____
_____
_____
_____
_____
_____
_____
_____
_____
_____
_____
_____
_____
_____
_____
_____
_____
_____
_____
_____
_____
_____
_____
_____
_____
_____
_____
_____
_____
_____
_____
_____
_____
_____
_____

The God-man Who Satisfies God's Desire and Fulfills His Good Pleasure

Scripture Reading: Psa. 15:1; 16:1-11

Day 1   I. Psalm 16 is "A Michtam of David" (title); the meaning of the Hebrew word *michtam* is uncertain, but some understand it to mean "a golden jewel (of a poem)."

II. Psalm 16 reveals that only Christ, the God-man, can satisfy God's desire and fulfill His good pleasure (Matt. 3:17; 17:5; cf. Psa. 15):

A. Only He—the very God who became a man, lived a human life full of the divine attributes expressed in human virtues, died, resurrected, and ascended to the right hand of God—is perfect according to the law and can sojourn in God's tabernacle and dwell with God on His holy mountain (v. 1).

B. In God's economy only the God-man Christ as the firstborn Son of God with His many brothers as the many sons of God (Rom. 8:29) can satisfy God's desire and fulfill His good pleasure.

Day 2   III. "Preserve me, O God, for I take refuge in You"
&   (Psa. 16:1):
Day 3   A. Christ took refuge in God and trusted in God's preservation.

B. The life that the Lord Jesus lived on earth was a life of continually trusting in God; His life was a trusting life (1 Pet. 2:23; Luke 23:46).

IV. "I say to Jehovah, You are my Lord; / No good have I beyond You" (Psa. 16:2):

A. When the Lord Jesus was a man on earth, He always held the attitude of recognizing God the Father as His Lord (Matt. 4:7, 10).

B. The Lord Jesus had no good (no blessing, no pleasure, and no enjoyment) beyond God the Father as His portion (cf. Luke 18:19; Isa. 53:2a).

V. "As for the saints who are on the earth, they are the excellent; / All my delight is in them" (Psa. 16:3):

   A. In His human living, the Lord Jesus loved God the Father (John 14:31), and He had His delight in the saints in God's kingdom.

   B. *The saints* implies the church, the Body of Christ; Christ delights in the saints, the excellent people on the earth, because they are the members who constitute His Body.

VI. **"The sorrows of them who bartered for some other god will be multiplied; / Their drink offerings of blood I will not offer, / Nor will I take up their names upon my lips" (Psa. 16:4):**

   A. Christ in His human living had nothing to do with other gods and their offerings, nor did He take up their names upon His lips.

   B. "Go away, Satan! For it is written, 'You shall worship the Lord your God, and Him only shall you serve'" (Matt. 4:10).

VII. **"Jehovah is the portion of my inheritance and of my cup; / You maintain my lot" (Psa. 16:5):**

   A. God is the portion of the inheritance and of the cup; *inheritance* refers to a possession, and *cup* refers to enjoyment.

   B. God the Father was the portion of the inheritance and of the cup to Christ as a man on earth; in Christ's human living, God was His possession and enjoyment.

VIII. **"The measuring lines have fallen on pleasant places for me; / Indeed the inheritance is beautiful to me" (v. 6):**

   A. Christ chose nothing for Himself; He left His destiny and all the choices to His Father (Matt. 11:25-30).

   B. Christ appreciated the possession given by God to Him under the measuring lines on pleasant places and the beautiful inheritance given to Him by God (Psa. 2:8; Rev. 11:15; cf. 2 Cor. 10:7-18).

IX. **"I will bless Jehovah, who counsels me; / Indeed in the nights my inward parts instruct me" (Psa. 16:7):**

   A. The Lord Jesus denied Himself and received the

Father's counsel, taking God the Father as His Counselor (Isa. 50:4).

B. The inward parts of Christ were one with God; when God counseled Him as a man, His inward parts instructed Him through His contact with God; this is the proper experience of a God-man (cf. Phil. 1:8).

Day 4   X. **"I have set Jehovah before me continually; / Because He is at my right hand, I shall not be shaken" (Psa. 16:8):**

A. Christ set God before Him continually to be His security, and He was not shaken, because God was at His right hand.

B. While the Lord Jesus was on earth, He was never alone, because the Father was always with Him (John 8:29).

XI. **"Therefore my heart rejoices and my glory exults; / Even my flesh dwells securely" (Psa. 16:9):**

A. In His death Christ's heart was rejoicing, and His glory, His spirit with His tongue, was exulting.

B. Christ was willing and happy to die for the accomplishment of God's economy.

C. The Lord Jesus rested physically in His burial, waiting to be resurrected.

XII. **"For You will not abandon my soul to Sheol, / Nor let Your Holy One see the pit" (v. 10):**

A. God would not abandon Christ's soul to Sheol (Hades), nor let His body see corruption, decay.

B. Christ's soul would be raised up from Hades, and His physical body would be resurrected from the tomb (Acts 2:31; Matt. 28:6; John 20:5-9).

Day 5   XIII. **"You will make known to me the path of life"**
&   **(Psa. 16:11a):**
Day 6

A. God would make known to Christ the path of life—resurrection.

B. In His incarnation Christ brought divinity into humanity; in His resurrection He brought humanity into divinity (John 1:14; Rom. 8:3; 1:2-4; Acts 13:33).

XIV. "In Your presence is fullness of joy; / At Your right hand there are pleasures forever" (Psa. 16:11b):

  A. Christ is in God's presence participating in fullness of joy; this indicates that Christ has ascended to the heavens to God's presence in order to enjoy His attainments and His obtainments (Acts 1:9-11; 2:36; 5:31; Phil. 2:9-11).

  B. In His ascension Christ is enjoying pleasures forever at God's right hand.

  C. Christ is at the right hand of God in His ascension for the accomplishment of God's eternal economy concerning the church, the Body of Christ (Eph. 1:20b-23).

Morning Nourishment

Psa.   O Jehovah, who may sojourn in Your tent? Who may
15:1   dwell on Your holy mountain?
Matt. While he was still speaking, behold, a bright cloud
17:5   overshadowed them, and behold, a voice out of the
       cloud, saying, This is My Son, the Beloved, in whom I
       have found My delight. Hear Him!

[Let us ask], "What kind of man may dwell with God for His heart's desire and good pleasure?" We may think that the man of good can dwell with God, but not the man of evil. Good and evil are our two lines. Teachers of philosophy and those of many religions would all say that if there is a God, only a good man, not an evil man, could dwell with Him. All of them would hold the same concept. But thank the Lord, in the Bible, which is His divine revelation, we have a pair of psalms, Psalms 15 and 16, to show us what kind of man God wants. God does not want an evil man or a good man. God rejects the good man as the evil man. They are of the same source, in the same nature, and in the same entity. They are in the same line and will arrive at the same end. Only a God-man can satisfy God's desire and fulfill His good pleasure. (*Life-study of the Psalms*, p. 87)

Today's Reading

Psalm 15:1 asks us, "O Jehovah, who may sojourn in Your tent? / Who may dwell on Your holy mountain?" David's answer is—the one who is perfect according to the law (vv. 2-5). But in the whole universe there is only one person who is perfect according to the law— Jesus Christ. There is no one else. Everyone else has broken the law. We have seen that David exalted the law so highly, but by his failure regarding Uriah, he broke the last five commandments (Exo. 20:13-17). He murdered, he committed adultery, he stole by robbing another of his wife, he lied to Uriah, and he coveted Uriah's wife (2 Sam. 11).

The last five commandments…were given by God with the requirement that man would have the human virtues to express the divine attributes. If there were no killing, fornication, stealing, lying, or coveting in the human race, the kingdom of the heavens would really be on this earth. Today the newspapers, however, report all the evil things that take place on earth day by day. The earth is filled with murder, fornication, stealing, lying, and coveting.

No one is perfect according to the law. Paul said in the New Testament that no flesh can be justified by God based upon man's keeping of the law (Rom. 3:20; Gal. 2:16). The only One who can and did keep the law is the One unveiled in Psalm 16. This One is the very God who became a man and lived a human life (vv. 1-8). In His human life, He kept the law perfectly. He lived a life full of human virtues expressing the divine attributes. Then He died (vv. 9-10) and was resurrected (vv. 10-11a). Now He is in ascension at the right hand of God (v. 11b & c). This is the One who can sojourn in God's tabernacle and dwell with God on His holy mountain.

Psalm 16:1-8 reveals the God-man, Christ, in His human living. He is not merely a good man, but a God-man. God became a man and lived on this earth....He was the very God living a human life in a small geographical area....He grew up in the small village of Nazareth in the despised place of Galilee for thirty years.... Then He came out to travel in His ministry. Of course, there was not the modern means of transportation which we enjoy today. Jesus had to travel mostly by foot within the land of Palestine.

The four Gospels show us the marvelous human living of this God-man. No biography can compare with Jesus' life. Millions of readers of these four Gospels have been inspired by the way in which Jesus Christ lived on earth. After His human living, He entered into death for three days and three nights. Then He came out of death and entered into resurrection. Finally, He ascended to the heavens where God the Father is. Today He is in ascension at the right hand of God the Father. Psalm 16 is a short psalm, but it covers such a wonderful person in His four stages: His human living, His death, His resurrection, and His ascension. (*Life-study of the Psalms,* pp. 72-73, 89)

Further Reading: Life-study of the Psalms, msg. 6

Enlightenment and inspiration: _____

_____

_____

_____

Morning Nourishment

Psa. Preserve me, O God, for I take refuge in You. I say to
16:1-4 Jehovah, You are my Lord; no good have I beyond
You; as for the saints who are on the earth, they are
the excellent; all my delight is in them. The sorrows of
them who bartered for some other *god* will be multiplied; their drink offerings of blood I will not offer, nor
will I take up their names upon my lips.

[Christ's] human living spontaneously implies His incarnation. If He had not been incarnated and did not have the human
nature with a human body, He could not have lived on earth.
Because He was altogether in humanity, He did not threaten anyone. Even the small children could come to Him (Luke 18:15-16).
He was so wonderful—because He was God born to be a man.
God, in this man, in this humanity, lived on earth.

His human living implies His incarnation in which He became
a man and brought divinity into humanity (John 1:14a)....Before
the incarnation, divinity was separate from humanity. But when
Jesus was born, divinity was brought into humanity, and divinity
and humanity were mingled together to produce a God-man.

Christ took refuge in God and trusted in God's preservation (Psa.
16:1). We may pray, "Lord Jesus, protect us; preserve us." When
Christ was a man on this earth, the very God in whom He trusted
was also His preservation. (*Life-study of the Psalms,* pp. 89-90)

Today's Reading

Christ took God as His Lord and had no good beyond God (Psa.
16:2). Today on earth everyone, even the most sinful person, is
claiming his rights. But the Lord Jesus, while He was a man on
this earth, did not claim any right for Himself. He took God as His
Lord. Every man needs God as his Lord. Without the Lord, we do
not know who our Possessor is. Our parents or our wives are not
our possessors. Christ the Lord is the One who owns us. He is our
Possessor. Christ in His human living had no good beyond God.
His good was uniquely God Himself as His portion.

Christ has delight in the saints, the excellent people on the earth (Psa. 16:3). *The saints* implies the church, the Body of Christ. Why does Christ delight in the saints? It is because the saints are the members that constitute His Body, the church....In Christ's view, we are a particular and excellent people. Christ delights in God's people, and He has made us excellent.

Christ in His human living had nothing to do with other gods and their offerings, nor did He take up their names upon His lips (Psa. 16:4). He would not mention the names of any idols. He even would not mention the names of the idol worshippers. That would contaminate His lips.

Christ took God as the portion of His inheritance and of His cup (Psa. 16:5). *Inheritance* refers to a possession, and *cup* refers to enjoyment. In Christ's human living, God became His possession and also His enjoyment. God was His inheritance and His cup. With the inheritance, there is a portion, and with the cup, there is also a portion. The portion of our inheritance and of our cup today is Christ. Furthermore, Christ trusted in God to maintain His lot (v. 5). Today the whole earth is a mess....We may think the earth is hopeless, but God still maintains it for Christ. Eventually, Christ will inherit the earth as His possession.

Christ appreciated the possession given by God to Him under the measuring lines on pleasant places and the beautiful inheritance given to Him by God (Psa. 16:6; 2:8; Rev. 11:15). This messy earth will become a pleasant globe to Christ when He comes back to inherit it.

Christ blessed God who counseled Him and was instructed by His inward parts in the nights through His contact with God (Psa. 16:7; Luke 6:12)....Christ set God before Him continually and was not shaken (cf. Psa. 15:5b) because God was at His right hand (Psa. 16:8; Acts 2:25). In John 8:29 the Lord said that while He was on this earth, He was never alone, because God the Father was always with Him. In Jesus' human living, God the Father was with Him. (*Life-study of the Psalms,* pp. 90-92)

Further Reading: Life-study of the Psalms, msg. 7

Enlightenment and inspiration: _____

_____
_____
_____

Morning Nourishment

Psa. **Jehovah is the portion of my inheritance and of my**
16:5-8 **cup; You maintain my lot. The measuring lines have**
fallen on pleasant places for me; indeed the inheri-
tance is beautiful to me. I will bless Jehovah, who
counsels me; indeed in the nights my inward parts
instruct me. I have set Jehovah before me continually;
because He is at my right hand, I shall not be shaken.

Let us consider Psalm 16 in more detail. The first section,
verses 1 through 8, describe the human life of Christ on earth.
These verses remove the veil to show us the living of this real man
by the name of Jesus. "Preserve me, O God, for I take refuge in You"
(v. 1). The life Jesus lived on this earth was a life of continual trust
in God. His life was a trusting life. Then verse 2 says, "I say to Jehovah, You are my Lord; / No good have I beyond You." This is the attitude of Jesus while He was on earth....Verse 3 says, "As for the
saints who are on the earth, they are the excellent; / All my delight
is in them." He considered all the saints so excellent; His delight
was in them. He trusted in God, and He loved all the saints. All
these points are abundantly proved in the four Gospels. (*Christ
and the Church Revealed and Typified in the Psalms,* pp. 38-39)

Today's Reading

In Psalm 16:4 and 5 the Lord Jesus continues, "The sorrows of
them who bartered for some other god will be multiplied; / Their
drink offerings of blood I will not offer, / Nor will I take up their
names upon my lips. / Jehovah is the portion of my inheritance and
of my cup; / You maintain my lot." This means that He had nothing
to do with any idol. His interest was in God and with God—nothing
else. Then verse 6 says, "The measuring lines have fallen on pleasant places for me; / Indeed the inheritance is beautiful to me." He
chose nothing for Himself; He left His destiny and all the choices to
His Father. Verse 7 says, "I will bless Jehovah, who counsels me; /
Indeed in the nights my inward parts instruct me." How much He
denied Himself! He trusted in the Father; He received the Father's
counsel. Then as a man He said, "I have set Jehovah before me

continually; / Because He is at my right hand, I shall not be shaken" (v. 8). We need to pray-read these eight verses and become intimately acquainted with the kind of life Christ lived while He was on earth as a man. This is the kind of life we need. (*Christ and the Church Revealed and Typified in the Psalms,* p. 39)

In Psalm 16:9-10 we see the revelation of the God-man, Christ, in His death (Acts 2:26-27)....Psalm 16:9a says that Christ's heart was rejoicing and His glory was exulting. This means His heart was rejoicing in Hades....In Christ's death His heart was rejoicing, and His spirit with His tongue was exulting.

Many saints come to the meetings and sit quietly. They are like the "marble Mary" outside some Catholic cathedrals. I would like to ask them, "Where is your spirit? Where is your mouth? Where is your tongue?" In the meetings their spirit is not exercised, their mouth is not exercised, and their tongue is not exercised. When we are in the meetings, we should exercise our spirit, our mouth, and our tongue to speak for the Lord. Then we will be glorious; we will be in glory. When we do not exercise in such a way, we are in a low condition. We need to exercise our spirit, our mouth, and our tongue to speak Christ to one another in the meetings. Then we are glorious because we are exercising the three parts of our glory: the spirit, the mouth, and the tongue.

Christ's heart rejoicing and His glory, His spirit with His tongue, exulting indicate that Christ was obedient to God even unto death, and that the death of a cross (Phil. 2:8). He was obedient unto death, not an ordinary death but a particular death, the death of the cross. This also indicates that Christ was willing and happy to die for the accomplishment of God's economy. He told us in John 10:17-18 that no one took His life away, but He laid it down. He also had the authority to take His life back. He died for the accomplishment of God's economy. (*Life-study of the Psalms,* pp. 92-93)

Further Reading: Christ and the Church Revealed and Typified in the Psalms, ch. 3

Enlightenment and inspiration: _____

_____

_____

_____

Morning Nourishment

Acts ...David says regarding Him, "I saw the Lord continually
2:25-27 before me, because He is on my right hand, that I may
not be shaken. Therefore my heart was made glad and
my tongue exulted; moreover, also my flesh will rest in
hope, because You will not abandon my soul to Hades,
nor will You permit Your Holy One to see corruption."

In His death, Christ's flesh (His physical body) dwelt securely
(Psa. 16:9b). This indicates that Christ's body was buried in a
secured tomb (Matt. 27:59-60). This also indicates that Christ was
resting physically in His burial waiting to be resurrected....His
soul went to Sheol (Hades) and remained there for three days
(Psa. 16:10a; Eph. 4:9)....He did not see corruption (decay) in His
physical body (Psa. 16:10b). This indicates His death and burial.
(*Life-study of the Psalms,* p. 93)

Today's Reading

Now we come to the third stage of Christ in Psalm 16—His resurrection (Psa. 16:10-11a; Acts 2:27-28a)....God would not abandon Christ's soul to Sheol, nor let Him as God's Holy One see corruption, decay (Psa. 16:10; Acts 2:31). This indicates that Christ's
soul would be raised up from Hades and also that Christ's physical
body would be resurrected from the tomb (Matt. 28:6; John 20:5-9).

God would make known to Christ the path of life—resurrection (Psa. 16:11a; Matt. 28:6). In His incarnation Christ brought
divinity into humanity; in His resurrection He brought humanity
into divinity. In His incarnation Christ made something divine,
human; in His resurrection He made something human, divine.

In resurrection Christ was also begotten of God to be the firstborn Son of God (Psa. 2:7; Acts 13:33; Rom. 8:29). Through His
incarnation Christ put on humanity. In His resurrection He
brought His human part into divinity to be begotten of God that
He could be the firstborn Son of God. In eternity past and before
His resurrection, He was the only begotten Son of God (John
3:16). But in resurrection the only begotten Son became the firstborn Son of God by having His humanity begotten of God.

In Christ's resurrection the believers were regenerated to be the many sons of God and the many brothers of Christ (1 Pet. 1:3; Heb. 2:10; Rom. 8:29). First Peter 1:3 says that through the resurrection of Christ, God regenerated us, all the believers. Actually, we were not regenerated at the time when we believed. That is merely according to our estimation. According to the divine fact, we all were regenerated together nearly two thousand years ago. When Christ in His humanity was begotten of God to be God's firstborn Son, all His believers were also begotten of God to be God's many sons. Thus, now through the resurrection of Christ, God has a group of sons, a corporate sonship. As sons of God, we need to realize that divinity was brought into our humanity and now our humanity is being brought into Christ's divinity. Christ was divinely human, and we are humanly divine. Thus, we are the same as He is in life and in nature, but not in the Godhead. (*Life-study of the Psalms,* pp. 94-95)

According to Peter's word in Acts 2:24-32, [Christ] was put to death and laid in the grave, and while He was in Hades, He was glad, for He said, "My heart was made glad and my tongue exulted" (v. 26). What is His "glory"? In Psalm 16 *glory* is often interpreted as referring to the innermost part of His being, the spirit. Jesus was saved out of death (Heb. 5:7), His heart was glad, and His spirit, the innermost part of His being, exulted. Peter translated *glory* as "tongue" because our spirit is the source of our praise, and our tongue is the means to express our praise....In the matter of praising God, our tongue has very much to do with our spirit. Whenever we praise the Lord, we must praise Him out of our spirit and by our tongue. Our heart is glad, our spirit exults, and our tongue praises. Then what about His body? His body was buried, but while His body was buried, His flesh rested in hope of resurrection....Peter tells us that [Psalm 16:10] means resurrection. (*Christ and the Church Revealed and Typified in the Psalms,* pp. 39-40)

Further Reading: Christ and the Church Revealed and Typified in the Psalms, ch. 3

Enlightenment and inspiration: _____

_____

_____

Morning Nourishment

Psa. For You will not abandon my soul to Sheol, nor let
16:10-11 Your Holy One see the pit. You will make known to me
the path of life; in Your presence is fullness of joy; at
Your right hand there are pleasures forever.
Acts "You have made known to me the ways of life; You will
2:28 make me full of gladness with Your presence."
Phil. Therefore also God highly exalted Him and bestowed
2:9 on Him the name which is above every name.

Psalm 16:11 says, "You will make known to me the path of
life; / In Your presence is fullness of joy; / At Your right hand there
are pleasures forever." If we have God's presence, we have fullness
of joy; if we are at His right hand, there are pleasures forever.
After Christ was resurrected, He was seated at the right hand of
God, where He enjoys pleasures forever. (*Christ and the Church
Revealed and Typified in the Psalms*, p. 40)

Today's Reading

Psalm 16 finally reveals the God-man, Christ, in His ascension (v. 11b & c; Acts 2:28b).

Christ is in God's presence participating in fullness of joy, indicating that Christ has ascended to the heavens for His attainments and His obtainments (Psa. 16:11b; Acts 1:11; Phil. 2:9-11).
In His ascension, among many other things, He attained to the
kingship, to the lordship, and to the ruling leadership and the
qualification of being a Savior to save others (Acts 5:31). He also
obtained many things in His ascension.

In His ascension Christ is enjoying pleasures forever in God's
right hand, indicating that Christ is also at the right hand of God
in His ascension to surpass all for the accomplishment of God's
eternal economy concerning the church, the Body of Christ (Psa.
16:11c; Eph. 1:20b-23). This is the wonderful God-man portrayed in Psalm 16.

We need to see the divine revelation of this wonderful person
in the Psalms. We may be like the blind man who was healed by

the Lord in Mark 8. After the Lord laid His hands on him, He asked this man if he saw anything. The blind man responded that he saw men as trees, walking. The Lord had to lay His hands upon this man again so that he could see clearly (vv. 22-25). We may be like this man because our eyes are not fully open yet. But as we get into the Psalms week by week, our eyes are becoming more open, and we are seeing more and more.

Our eyes need to be opened until we have a full vision, a full revelation, concerning this wonderful person. He is the Word of God, even God Himself. In eternity past, He was full of divinity without any humanity. But one day in time He came to be incarnated and put on humanity. He became a God-man with a human body and lived on this earth for thirty-three and a half years. Then He entered into death to accomplish God's redemption according to God's eternal plan, God's economy.

Christ came out of death and entered into resurrection. In this resurrection He brought His humanity into divinity to be begotten of God to become God's firstborn Son, and God regenerated all His believers to be God's many sons. Furthermore, in resurrection, He became a life-giving Spirit (1 Cor. 15:45b). As the life-giving Spirit, He is now within His believers as their life and their life supply.

He ascended to the heavens to attain many positions and to obtain many qualifications. In His ascension He became the Lord, the King, the Ruler, the Savior, and even the Christ for the accomplishment of God's economy that God could produce an organism, that is, the Body of Christ in resurrection as the church.

This is the Christ revealed in Psalm 16. This is the man that can sojourn in God's temple and dwell on God's holy mountain. Such a man is not a good man according to the law, but a God-man according to God Himself as the life and life supply. (*Life-study of the Psalms*, pp. 95-96)

Further Reading: Life-study of the Psalms, msg. 7

Enlightenment and inspiration: _____

_____

_____

Morning Nourishment

Psa. O Jehovah, who may sojourn in Your tent? Who may
15:1 dwell on Your holy mountain?
16:11 ...In Your presence is fullness of joy; at Your right
hand there are pleasures forever.

The real answer [to the question in Psalm 15:1] is in Psalm 16.
Then what about [the answer in] Psalm 15? That answer is according to the human and religious concept. The answer according to the heavenly vision is the One revealed in Psalm 16. Such a
One will sojourn in God's tent and dwell on His holy mountain. He
is there now; He is in the presence of God; He is at the right hand of
God. Which one? The One who took refuge in God, the One who
lived in the presence of God, the One who was put to death, who
was resurrected by God, and who ascended to God's right hand.
This is the One who can dwell in the tabernacle of God. (*Christ
and the Church Revealed and Typified in the Psalms,* p. 40)

Today's Reading

From Psalm 1 to Psalm 16, there is a history which...begins in
Psalm 1 with a man appreciating the law, treasuring the keeping
of the law, and highly appraising the keeper of the law. Then in
Psalm 2, God came in to declare that Christ was His Anointed.
God anointed Him and installed Him to be the King. God also begot
Him in His humanity to be the firstborn Son of God. Thus, we all
have to take refuge in Him, to believe into Him. We also have to
kiss Him, to love Him. This is the second step of the history.

After Psalm 2 was written, David...committed...adultery
with Uriah's wife and murdered Uriah (2 Sam. 11)....By that terrible sin, he broke the last five commandments (Exo. 20:13-17).
He murdered Uriah, committed fornication, robbed Uriah of his
wife, lied to Uriah, and coveted Uriah's wife.

The title of Psalm 3 says that this psalm was written when
David was fleeing from his son Absalom. David fled from his son
because his son rebelled against him. This rebellion was the issue
of David's sin of fornication and murder.

David was exposed to the uttermost....It is hard to believe that such a godly servant of God as David could commit such a terrible sin....God allowed that to happen. God kept His preserving, protecting, and sustaining hand away from David for a time. David thought he kept the law, but God arranged an environment to show him that he could not keep the law. An environment was there that fit David's sinful flesh, allowing his flesh to come out and fully expose him.

[David] was exposed, and later he was on the test with Absalom's rebellion. When Absalom was pursuing him, David prayed the prayers recorded in Psalms 3—7....In the light of God's New Testament economy...these psalms should not be taken as models for our prayer. In them we see David's sufferings, his desire to be avenged of his adversaries, and his self-righteousness. We do not see any repentance, confession of his fault, or self-condemnation. This is the history of the one who appreciated the law and who was exposed. There is no hint or indication that he was humbled, that he was full of self-denial, or that he was self-condemned. He was on the test during Absalom's rebellion, and the testing did not bring out anything positive in these psalms.

[Psalm 8] is David's inspired praise of the excellency of Christ. ...[Then] Psalms 9—14...show us David's human concept concerning God's judgment on his enemies and his concept concerning man's condition before God. Then Psalm 15 speaks of David's concept of a perfect man according to the law being able to dwell with God for God's heart's desire. But in Psalm 16, there is the divine revelation that the only one who can dwell with God for God's heart's desire is the God-man, Christ. The God-man Christ in His human living, His death, His resurrection, and His ascension is the centrality and universality of the economy of God, the man who may dwell with God for His heart's desire and good pleasure. I hope that we can keep in mind the history of these sixteen psalms. Then we can understand their real significance. (*Life-study of the Psalms*, pp. 96-98)

Further Reading: Life-study of the Psalms, msg. 7

Enlightenment and inspiration: _____

_____

_____

_____

Hymns, #1082

1   The living of Christ when He sojourned on earth,
    The sixteenth Psalm shows us, was wholly of worth.
    His attitudes, choices, and interests all tell
    The man who in God's tabernacle may dwell.

2   "Preserve me, O God, for in Thee I confide"—
    In God He took refuge whate'er did betide.
    "O Thou art my Lord, I've no good beyond Thee"—
    He spoke in Himself unto God constantly.

3   "As for all the saints who are dwelling on earth,"
    To Him they're the people of excellent worth.
    Of them He has said He has all His delight—
    In proving this all the four Gospels unite.

4   "The Lord is my portion, the Lord is my cup"—
    For everything He to the Father looked up.
    "The Lord I will bless who my counsel doth give"—
    Himself He denied and by God's word did live.

5   His heart thus was glad and His spirit rejoiced,
    And e'en in His death praise to God could be voiced;
    His soul God would never abandon to hell,
    But in resurrection His body would dwell.

6   God raised Him, and He with God's glory was crowned;
    Then fulness of joy in God's presence He found.
    E'en now at the Father's right hand is His seat,
    Where flowing forever are pleasures complete.

Composition for prophecy with main point and sub-points: _____

_____
_____
_____
_____
_____
_____
_____
_____
_____
_____
_____
_____
_____
_____
_____
_____
_____
_____
_____
_____
_____
_____
_____
_____
_____
_____
_____
_____
_____
_____
_____
_____
_____
_____
_____
_____
_____
_____
_____
_____
_____

Christ in His Redeeming Death and Church-producing Resurrection

Scripture Reading: Psa. 22; Matt. 27:45-46; Heb. 2:10-12

Day 1   I. **The subject of Psalm 22 is the Christ who has passed through His redeeming death and entered into His church-producing resurrection.**

II. **Psalm 22:1-21 gives a detailed picture of Christ in His suffering of death (cf. Isa. 53), as typified by David in his suffering:**

A. The question in Psalm 22:1 was spoken by David in his suffering, but it became a prophecy concerning Christ in His suffering of His redeeming death.

B. Verses 6 through 8 display Christ's suffering unto death through men's reproach, despising, deriding, sneering, head-shaking, and mocking.

C. Verses 9 through 11 show that while people were mocking Him and deriding Him, Christ trusted in God for deliverance, that is, for resurrection; He intended definitely to die and expected to be delivered from death, that is, to be resurrected from the dead (Luke 18:31-33; Heb. 5:7).

D. Psalm 22:12-18 depicts in vivid detail how Christ passed through His suffering of crucifixion (Mark 15:16-37).

Day 2   E. God judged Christ and put Him into death for our redemption (Psa. 22:15):

1. On the one hand, man crucified the Lord Jesus; on the other hand, God killed Him:

   a. In the first three hours that Christ was on the cross, He was persecuted by men for doing God's will.

   b. In the last three hours, Christ was our Substitute, He became sin on our behalf, and He died a vicarious death to redeem us from our sins and from God's judgment (2 Cor. 5:21; 1 Pet. 3:18; 1 Cor. 15:3).

2. All the sin of the world was laid on Christ as the Lamb of God; God judged Him and put Him into death for our redemption (Isa. 53:6b, 10a; 1 Pet. 2:24a; John 1:29).

Day 3   F. On the cross Christ was forsaken by God (Psa. 22:1; Matt. 27:45-46):

1. While Christ was on the earth, God the Father was with Him all the time, but at a certain point in His crucifixion, God forsook Him (John 8:29; Matt. 27:45-46).

2. When the Lord Jesus died on the cross under God's judgment, He had God within Him essentially as His divine being; nevertheless, He was forsaken by the righteous and judging God economically (1:20; 3:16-17):

   a. The Lord Jesus had been born of the Spirit; thus, the Spirit was one of the two essences of His being (1:20; Luke 1:35).

   b. Before the Spirit of God descended and came upon the Lord Jesus, He already had the Spirit of God within Him (Matt. 3:16).

   c. On the cross Christ, the God-man, presented Himself to God as the all-inclusive sacrifice through the eternal Spirit (Heb. 9:14).

   d. After God had counted Christ as a sinner to be our Substitute and had accepted His offering, God, as the Holy Spirit who had come upon Him, forsook Him (Matt. 27:46).

3. Although God as the Spirit left the Lord Jesus economically, Christ nevertheless died as the Son of God, a God-man; hence, in His death there is a divine and eternal element (Acts 20:28; 1 John 1:7; Heb. 9:12).

Day 4 **III. After passing through His redeeming death, Christ entered into His church-producing resurrection (Psa. 22:22-31):**

A. Verses 22 through 31 refer to Christ in His resurrection, as typified by Solomon in his kingly reign.

B. *I* in verse 22a is the resurrected Christ who declares
the Father's name to His brothers (Heb. 2:12):
1. It was in His resurrection that Christ called
   His disciples His brothers, for in God's eternal view His disciples were regenerated and
   became God's sons in Christ's resurrection
   (John 20:17; Matt. 28:10; 1 Pet. 1:3).
2. In His resurrection Christ Himself was begotten to be God's firstborn Son (Psa. 2:7; Acts
   13:33) and became the life-giving Spirit (1 Cor.
   15:45b), and all God's chosen and redeemed
   people were regenerated to be the many sons
   of God, the many brothers of Christ (Heb.
   2:10-12; Rom. 8:29).
C. In Psalm 22:22b the assembly signifies the church,
   indicating that the Lord's brothers constitute
   the church; thus, His resurrection is the church-
   producing resurrection (Heb. 2:10-12):

Day 5

1. The church is a living composition of the many
   sons of God, who are the many brothers of
   Christ, brought forth in His resurrection
   (vv. 10-12).
2. As the many brothers of Christ, we are the
   same as the firstborn Son; He is divine and
   human, and we are human and divine, and thus
   the church is both human and divine—an
   organism with two lives and two natures combined and mingled together (v. 11; 1:6; Rom.
   8:29; cf. Lev. 2).
D. In Psalm 22:22 *You* and *Your* refer to the Father:
1. In resurrection Christ declared the Father's
   name to His brothers and praised the Father
   in the church (Heb. 2:12).

Day 6

2. The praise in Psalm 22:22 is the firstborn Son's
   praising of the Father within the Father's many
   sons in the church meetings (Heb. 2:10, 12):
   a. It is not that the Son praises the Father apart
      from us and alone; rather, He praises with-
      in us and with us through our praising.

b. When we, the many sons of God, meet as the church and praise the Father, the first-born Son praises the Father in our praising (v. 12b; cf. Matt. 26:30).

E. The church ushers in Christ's kingdom for Christ to rule over the nations; the church, produced by Christ's resurrection, is the reality of the kingdom and a precursor to the manifestation of the kingdom in the millennium (Psa. 22:27-28; Matt. 16:18-19; Rom. 14:17).

F. Jehovah as Christ will rule over the nations in the millennial kingdom (Psa. 22:28; 2:8-9; Rev. 19:15; 20:4, 6).

G. The believers are the seed of Christ, and their declaring the Lord's righteousness (justification, salvation) to a coming generation refers to the preaching of the gospel (Psa. 22:30-31).

Morning Nourishment

Luke 18:31-33 ...Behold we are going up to Jerusalem, and all things which have been written through the prophets regarding the Son of Man will be accomplished, for He will be delivered up to the Gentiles and will be mocked and outrageously treated and spat upon; and when they have scourged *Him*, they will kill Him; and on the third day He will rise.

The first twenty-one verses of Psalm 22 cover the death of Christ, the crucifixion of Christ, and the last ten verses cover His resurrection. Isaiah 53 is a particular chapter on Christ's death in detail. Psalm 22 is another chapter...on the death of Christ which is full of details. We need these two chapters in order to see a thorough, detailed picture of Christ's death.

The subject of Psalm 22 is the Christ who has passed through the redeeming death and entered into the church-producing resurrection. His death is for redeeming, and His resurrection is for producing the church. (*Life-study of the Psalms,* p. 128)

Today's Reading

Psalm 22:1-21 show[s] us Christ passing through the redeeming death....Verse 1 says, "My God, my God, why have You forsaken me?" This word was spoken by David in his suffering. Actually, it became a prophecy concerning Christ in His suffering of His redeeming death. It was quoted by the Lord Jesus while He was suffering the crucifixion (Matt. 27:46).

Verses 2-5 are the continuation of David's groaning prayer, which turned from groaning to praising....Beginning from verse six, the voice changes to another person, to Christ. This is the way the Psalms were written. While David was speaking, eventually Christ came in to speak in his speaking.

In Psalm 22 we see the suffering David typifying Christ passing through His death (vv. 1a, 6-21)....The suffering of Christ unto death was through men's reproach, despising, deriding, sneering, head shaking, and mocking (vv. 6-8; Heb. 13:13b; Isa. 53:3; Luke 23:11; Mark 15:29-32; Matt. 27:39-44). ...Each of [these words] has a particular meaning to describe what the Lord suffered on the cross,...[but] we have a tendency to take everything for granted.

The word *reproach* is also used in Hebrews 13:13, which says, "Let us therefore go forth unto Him outside the camp, bearing His reproach." This indicates that we need to come outside the camp of religion to follow the suffering Jesus. To bear the Lord's reproach is to bear His disgrace or shame. To despise is to look down on with contempt and scorn. To deride is to make fun of or laugh at in contempt. To sneer is to smile or laugh with facial contortions that express scorn or contempt. When Christ was on the cross, the ridiculers also shook, or wagged, their heads (Psa. 22:7b; Matt. 27:39; Mark 15:29), saying, "He committed himself to Jehovah; let Him rescue him" (Psa. 22:8a). To mock is to hold up to scorn or contempt and to imitate or mimic in derision. All these things were suffered by the Lord Jesus Christ while He was nailed on the cross. Groups of people reproached Him, despised Him, derided Him, sneered at Him, shook their heads at Him, and mocked Him.

Psalm 22:9-11 shows that Christ trusted in God for deliverance. While people were mocking Him and deriding Him, He was trusting in God. Deliverance here is resurrection. He intended definitely to die and expected to be delivered from death, that is, to be resurrected from the dead.

Psalm 22:12-18 shows how Christ passed through the suffering of crucifixion. The Jewish people did not have the practice of crucifying criminals. This was a practice of the heathen (Ezra 6:11) adopted by the Romans for the execution of slaves and heinous criminals. As the Lamb of God, Christ was crucified for our redemption (John 1:29; Heb. 9:12).

On the cross, He was poured out like water (v. 14a). Isaiah 53:12 says that He poured out His soul. We cannot fully realize the tremendous amount of suffering which the Lord experienced on the cross. (*Life-study of the Psalms,* pp. 128-131)

Further Reading: Christ and the Church Revealed and Typified in the Psalms, ch. 4; *Life-study of Matthew,* msg. 70

Enlightenment and inspiration: _____

_____

_____

Morning Nourishment

Psa.   My strength is dried up like a shard, and my tongue is
22:15 stuck to my jaws; You have put me in the dust of death.
2 Cor. Him who did not know sin He made sin on our behalf
5:21   that we might become the righteousness of God in
       Him.

Years ago, I read an article describing how the children of
Israel slew the lamb during the Passover. They took two wooden
bars and formed a cross. They tied two legs of the lamb at the foot
of the cross and fastened the other outstretched legs to the cross-
bar. Then they slew the lamb so that all its blood was shed, for
they needed all of the blood to sprinkle on their doorframes (Exo.
12:7). The way the Passover lamb was killed is a picture of
Christ's crucifixion on the cross as the Lamb of God. (*Life-study of
the Psalms,* p. 131)

Today's Reading

While Christ was being crucified on the cross, many fierce
men, signified by mighty bulls, encompassed Him (Psa. 22:12).
They opened their mouth at Him like a ravening and roaring lion
(v. 13). Evil men, signified by dogs, surrounded Him, and a congre-
gation of evildoers enclosed Him (v. 16a-b).

Psalm 22:16c says that they pierced His hands and feet (Zech.
12:10; John 19:37; Rev. 1:7). Charles Wesley in one of his hymns
spoke of the "five bleeding wounds" which Christ received on Cal-
vary (*Hymns,* #300). His two hands, His two feet, and His side (John
19:34) were pierced by the Roman soldiers who executed Him.

They divided His garments to themselves, and for His clothing
they cast lots (Psa. 22:18; John 19:23-24). In His crucifixion, the
Lord's right to be clothed was stripped from Him, along with His
life. They made the Lord Jesus altogether naked in order to have
a public, shameful display.

Psalm 22:17b says that they looked, they stared at Him. The
evildoers were staring at the Lord Jesus with contempt and
hatred while He was on the cross.

Verse 14b says that all His bones were out of joint. This was because He could not hold up the weight of His body hanging on the cross. His bones being out of joint caused Him great agony and pain.

Also, He counted all His bones (v. 17a). His heart was like wax melted within Him (v. 14c-d). His strength was dried up like a shard (v. 15a; John 19:28), a piece of broken pottery. His tongue was stuck to His jaws (Psa. 22:15b). God had put Him in the dust of death (v. 15c; Phil. 2:8b). He was put to death by God. On the one hand, it was man crucifying Him, killing Him, but eventually it was God who put Him into death. Actually, God killed Jesus. If Jesus had been killed only by man, He could never have been our Redeemer. He would have been merely a martyr. But God judged Him and put Him into death for our redemption (Isa. 53:4, 10).

Christ asked God to deliver Him from death (Psa. 22:19-21). Hebrews 5:7 says that Christ cried to God for God's deliverance, that is, for God to raise Him up from the dead.

Psalm 22:1 shows that on the cross Christ was forsaken by God (v. 1a; Matt. 27:45-46). The beginning of Psalm 22 speaks of this, but in the sequence of events on the cross, Christ cried out "My God, My God, why have You forsaken Me?" at about the ninth hour, or 3:00 P.M. (Matt. 27:46). This was at the end of His crucifixion. Christ was hanging on the cross for six hours, from the third hour, 9:00 A.M. (Mark 15:25), to the ninth hour, 3:00 P.M. In the first three hours, He was persecuted by men for doing God's will; in the last three hours, He was judged by God to accomplish our redemption. It was during the last three hours that God counted Him as our Substitute who suffered for our sin (Isa. 53:10).

Darkness fell over all the land (Matt. 27:45) because our sin and sins and all negative things were being dealt with on the cross. Isaiah 53:6 says that God laid all of our sins upon Christ. He was forsaken by God for our sins (1 Cor. 15:3), becoming sin on our behalf (2 Cor. 5:21) to be judged by God as our Substitute. (*Life-study of the Psalms,* pp. 131-132)

Further Reading: Life-study of Luke, msgs. 51-53

Enlightenment and inspiration: _____

_____

_____

Morning Nourishment

Psa. My God, my God, why have You forsaken me? *Why are*
22:1 *You* so far from saving me, *from* the words of my
groaning?

Heb. ...Through His own blood, entered once for all into
9:12 the *Holy of* Holies, obtaining an eternal redemption.
14 How much more will the blood of Christ, who through
the eternal Spirit offered Himself without blemish to
God, purify our conscience from dead works to serve
the living God?

When the Lord Jesus cried, "My God, My God, why have You forsaken Me?" it was during the time He was bearing our sins (1 Pet.
2:24), being made sin for us (2 Cor. 5:21) and taking the place of
sinners (1 Pet. 3:18). This means that God judged Him as our Substitute for our sins. In the sight of God, Christ became a great sinner. Concerning this, 2 Corinthians 5:21 says, "Him who did not
know sin He made sin on our behalf." When did God make Christ
sin for us? Was it during the whole period of the thirty-three and a
half years of the Lord's life on earth? No. If the Lord Jesus had
been made sin by God during all of His life, then God could not
have been with Him, and God could not have had His delight in
Him. I believe that it was during the last three hours Christ was
on the cross, from twelve o'clock until three o'clock in the after-
noon, the hours when darkness came over the whole land, that
God made Him sin. God made Christ not only our Substitute; God
even made Him sin on our behalf. (*Life-study of Mark,* p. 418)

Today's Reading

Because Christ was our Substitute and was made sin in the
sight of God, God judged Him. I believe that it was during this
time, at about the ninth hour, that the anointing Spirit left the
Lord Jesus.

We have pointed out strongly that before the Holy Spirit, the
anointing Spirit, descended upon the Lord Jesus, He already had
the divine essence within Him as one of two essences of His being.
Now we need to see that the divine essence never left Him. Even

when He was on the cross crying out, "My God, My God, why have You forsaken Me?" He still had the divine essence. Then who left Him? The anointing Spirit through whom He presented Himself to God left Him. After God accepted Christ as the all-inclusive offering, the anointing Spirit left Him. But although the anointing Spirit left Him, He still had the divine essence.

The death of the Lord Jesus was not merely the death of a man; it was the death of a God-man. For this reason, His death has eternal effectiveness. The Lord's death has eternal power for our redemption. Otherwise, it would not be possible for one man to die for so many people. An individual person is limited because a human being is not eternal. If the Lord had died merely as a man, His death would have been limited in its effectiveness. He could have been a Substitute for one person, but not for millions of persons. However, the Lord's death was the death of a God-man and therefore was an eternal death accomplishing eternal redemption, redemption with eternal power and effectiveness.

Before the Holy Spirit descended upon the Lord Jesus, the Lord already had the divine essence. When He was baptized, He was baptized as a God-man. After His baptism, the Holy Spirit descended upon Him as the God-man to anoint Him for His ministry. For three and a half years He ministered by this Spirit. Then on the cross He presented Himself as the God-man to be the all-inclusive sacrifice through the eternal Spirit. After God had counted Him as a sinner to be our Substitute, even making Him sin for us, and had accepted His offering, God as the Holy Spirit who had come upon Him forsook Him. Nevertheless, the Lord was still a God-man and died as such. This means that even though God as the Spirit left the Lord, the Lord died not merely as a man but as a God-man. Therefore, there is in His death a divine and eternal element. His death has accomplished eternal redemption with eternal power and effectiveness. (*Life-study of Mark,* pp. 418-419)

Further Reading: Life-study of Mark, msgs. 48-49

Enlightenment and inspiration: _____

_____

_____

_____

Morning Nourishment

Heb. For both He who sanctifies and those who are being
2:11-12 sanctified are all of One, for which cause He is not
ashamed to call them brothers, saying, "I will declare
Your name to My brothers; in the midst of the church
I will sing hymns of praise to You."

After passing through His redeeming death, Christ entered into
the church-producing resurrection (Psa. 22:22-31)....It was in His
resurrection that Christ called His disciples His brothers. Psalm
22:22 says, "I will declare Your name to my brothers; / In the midst
of the assembly I will praise You." In this verse "I" is the resurrected Christ who declares the Father's name to His brothers. If
He had remained in death, He could not have declared God the
Father's name to His brothers. (*Life-study of the Psalms*, p. 133)

Today's Reading

Christ was on the earth with His disciples for the three and a
half years of His earthly ministry, but He never called them His
brothers until the morning of the day He resurrected. On that
day, the Lord told Mary, "Go to My brothers and say to them, I
ascend to My Father and your Father, and My God and your God"
(John 20:17). This means that the disciples became God's sons in
Christ's resurrection. Before His resurrection the disciples were
not His brothers because they had not been regenerated. But when
Christ was resurrected, all the believers, including you and me,
were resurrected with Him and in Him (Eph. 2:6). Through His
resurrection, we were regenerated (1 Pet. 1:3). Resurrection was
a big delivery, a big birth. Acts 13:33 says that resurrection was a
birth to Christ. Christ was the only begotten Son of God (John
3:16), but in resurrection He was begotten as the firstborn Son of
God with many brothers (Rom. 8:29), many sons of God.

First Peter 1:3 says that through Christ's resurrection, God
regenerated all of us believers. Some may think that they were
regenerated at a certain point in time a few years ago. But actually we all were regenerated at the same time before we were
born....The resurrection of Christ was a delivery of millions of

sons of God at the same time. He was the firstborn Son of God in resurrection, and we followed Him to be the many sons of God. On the day of His resurrection, He could say that His Father is our Father because He and we were all born of the same Father. We, His believers, His disciples, became His brothers.

The second half of Psalm 22:22 is very meaningful. It says, "In the midst of the assembly I will praise You." "The assembly" is the church, and "You" is the Father God. At the Lord's table we follow the Lord's pattern in praising the Father. After we remember the Lord by taking the bread and the wine, we follow the Lord to praise the Father, to worship the Father. According to logic, verse 22b should say, "In the midst of *them* I will praise You." But the Lord changed the pronoun *them* to *the assembly*. "My brothers" became the church, the assembly. The Lord's brothers constitute the church (Heb. 2:11-12).

In resurrection Christ declared the Father's name to His brothers and praised the Father in the church. His resurrection is the church-producing resurrection. Hebrews 2:11-12 says, "For both He who sanctifies and those who are being sanctified are all of One, for which cause He is not ashamed to call them brothers, saying, 'I will declare Your name to My brothers; in the midst of the church I will sing hymns of praise to You.'" He who sanctifies is Christ, and those who are being sanctified are we believers. We are both of One, that is, out of one Father. Hebrews 2:12 is a quotation of Psalm 22:22. (*Life-study of the Psalms*, pp. 133-135)

The church is composed of the many sons of God who are the many brothers of Christ in resurrection. It is a corporate partnership with Christ, the firstborn Son of God, to participate in the Father's life, nature, and being. In the church, the Father is praised by His firstborn Son within His many sons. This is the church. Now we have seen something regarding the many sons, the many brothers, and the church. (*Life-study of Hebrews*, p. 140)

Further Reading: Christ and the Church Revealed and Typified in the Psalms, ch. 5; *Life-study of Hebrews*, msg. 11

Enlightenment and inspiration: _____

_____

_____

_____

Morning Nourishment

Psa.   I will declare Your name to my brothers; in the midst
22:22 of the assembly I will praise You.
Rom.   Because those whom He foreknew, He also predesti-
8:29   nated *to be* conformed to the image of His Son, that
       He might be the Firstborn among many brothers.

What is the church? The church is a corporate composition of
the brothers of the firstborn Son of God....The only begotten Son
of God had divinity without humanity. Although He had the divine
nature, He did not have the human nature. But the firstborn Son
of God has both the divine nature and the human nature. The
brothers are not the brothers of the only Begotten, but the brothers of the firstborn Son of God. We are the same as the Firstborn.
He is divine and human, and we are human and divine. The firstborn Son has humanity as well as divinity and all of His brothers
are the same as He is. (*Life-study of Hebrews,* p. 132)

Today's Reading

The church is not only a gathering of real believers; it is a body,
the Body of Christ. If you gather many chairs together, the chairs
cannot become a body....As everybody knows, a body is an organism with life. It has life tissues, life cells, life nature, life shape,
life ability, and life function. The church is deeper, higher, and
more profound than just a gathering.

The Lord has shown us the real significance of the church.
Praise Him that He has granted us to see that the church has two
natures—the human nature and the divine nature. The church
has two lives. These lives are not only combined but are also mingled together. The church is an organism with two natures and
with two lives combined and mingled together. This is marvelous!
Do you realize that the church has two lives? Do you realize that
the church has two natures? Do you realize that the firstborn Son
of God has two lives and two natures, that He is not only the Son
of God, but also the Son of Man? The Firstborn has all of the
divine attributes as well as all of the human virtues. What we

have is not just a little humility or submission. This rich store is much more profound than this. It is unlimited and immeasurable, filled with the divine attributes and the human virtues. The church is such an organism. It is the Body of Christ.

Quite often bad news comes to me about a church in a certain place. Someone may say, "The church there is not good. It has problems." I do not like to hear things like this, because my concept of the church is based upon my faith. I believe that every church is wonderful. There is not a church that is not good. Although you may think that a certain church is not good, after a period of time that church becomes very different. Why? Because the church is organic. It grows. Your body may be quite tired, but after a while it is invigorated. It changes by life because it is an organism. The churches in the Lord's recovery are organic. Never believe that the church in a certain locality is not good. The church is wonderful because it is an organism that grows. Never forget that the church is a living corporation of all the brothers of the firstborn Son of God. The church is neither physical nor organizational; it is altogether of life—the divine life and the uplifted, resurrected human life. Nothing is richer than life. The best life in the universe is the divine life, and the second best life is the human life. The human life that we have today for the church is not the natural human life but the uplifted, resurrected human life. We have such a life! This human life plus the divine life is the life of the church. It is in such a profound way that the church is revealed in this book. The church is a living composition of all the sons of God, a living corporation of all the brothers of the firstborn Son of God. (*Life-study of Hebrews,* pp. 133-134)

You and *Your* in Psalm 22:22 refer to the Father. In resurrection Christ declared the Father's name to His brothers and praised the Father in the church (Heb. 2:12 and footnote 3). (Psa. 22:22, footnote 3)

Further Reading: The Conclusion of the New Testament, msg. 39; *Life-study of Hebrews,* msg. 12*

Enlightenment and inspiration: _____

_____

_____

_____

Morning Nourishment

Psa. **For the kingdom is Jehovah's, and He rules among**
22:28 **the nations.**
30 **A seed will serve Him; that which concerns the**
Lord will be told to a *coming* generation.

To us, God is no longer merely the creating God but also the begetting Father. He has begotten us. He has imparted His life, His nature, and even His being into our being. This is what it means to declare the Father's name.

After declaring the Father's name, the Son sings hymns of praise to Him in the midst of the church. I do not believe that this prophecy means that the firstborn Son of God sang hymns of praise to the Father in the church only once. Rather, I believe that it means throughout all the centuries the firstborn Son has been continually singing hymns of praise unto the Father in the church. How does He do this? He does it in all of His brothers. I have the full assurance that right now He is inside of us. Since He is in us, He sings praises unto the Father in our singing. His singing is in our singing. When we sing, He sings because He is within our singing. When we sing hymns to the Father from our spirit, He sings with us in our spirit. This is wonderful. (*Life-study of Hebrews*, p. 139)

Today's Reading

The church on earth today is one corporate Body with the firstborn Son of God. In the meetings of the church, the firstborn Son of God sings praise to the Father. Whenever we come to the meetings, we must open our mouths to praise the Father. If we do this immediately, we cooperate with the indwelling firstborn Son of God. Do you want to gain more of the firstborn Son? If you do, you need to praise the Father. The more we praise the Father, the more we gain the firstborn Son. The more we sing, the more He sings in our singing. The best way to have Christ work together with us is by singing praises to the Father. According to our experiences, many of us can testify that this is so. In some of the church meetings we did much singing to the Father. That was the time when we enjoyed Christ so much.

We even had the sensation that He was singing in our singing.

Christ has made the Father known to us as the source of life. Now in all the church meetings He is waiting for the opportunity to cooperate with us in singing praises to the Father. The best way for us to give Him this cooperation is to open our spirit and sing praise to the Father. The more we sing, the more we shall enjoy His singing. When we praise the Father, we enjoy Christ. We are one with Christ in praising the Father in the church meetings. The more we praise the Father in the church meetings, the more He praises the Father in our praising, and the more we enjoy Him and gain Him. (*Life-study of Hebrews,* pp. 139-140)

Christ's church ushers in His kingdom for Him to rule over the nations. Psalm 22:27-28 says, "All the ends of the earth / Will remember and return to Jehovah, / And all families of the nations / Will worship before You; / For the kingdom is Jehovah's, / And He rules among the nations." Christ has the kingdom, and He will rule among the nations.

The church ushers in the kingdom. Actually, the church is the reality of the kingdom and a precursor of the manifestation of the kingdom. Today the church is the kingdom. Romans 14:17 says the church life is the kingdom life, the kingdom of God. But this is a precursor of the coming kingdom, just as the tabernacle was a precursor of the temple. Today's church life is a miniature, a precursor, of the coming kingdom of one thousand years. The church is produced by the resurrection of Christ, and the kingdom will be ushered in by the church. (*Life-study of the Psalms,* p. 135)

Jehovah as Christ will rule over the nations in the millennial kingdom (Psa. 2:8-9; Rev. 19:15; 20:4, 6). (Psa. 22:28, footnote 1)

The believers are the seed of Christ, and their declaring the Lord's righteousness (justification, salvation) to a coming generation (Psa. 22:30-31) refers to the preaching of the gospel. (Psa. 22:30, footnote 1)

Further Reading: Life-study of the Psalms, msg. 10; *The Conclusion of the New Testament,* msg. 209

Enlightenment and inspiration: _____

_____

_____

_____

Hymns, #203

1 In the bosom of the Father,
   Ere the ages had begun,
Thou wast in the Father's glory,
   God's unique begotten Son.
When to us the Father gave Thee,
   Thou in person wast the same,
All the fulness of the Father
   In the Spirit to proclaim.

2 By Thy death and resurrection,
   Thou wast made God's firstborn Son;
By Thy life to us imparting,
   Was Thy duplication done.
We, in Thee regenerated,
   Many sons to God became;
Truly as Thy many brethren,
   We are as Thyself the same.

3 Once Thou wast the only grain, Lord,
   Falling to the earth to die,
That thru death and resurrection
   Thou in life may multiply.
We were brought forth in Thy nature
   And the many grains became;
As one loaf we all are blended,
   All Thy fulness to proclaim.

4 We're Thy total reproduction,
   Thy dear Body and Thy Bride,
Thine expression and Thy fulness,
   For Thee ever to abide.
We are Thy continuation,
   Thy life-increase and Thy spread,
Thy full growth and Thy rich surplus,
   One with Thee, our glorious Head.

Composition for prophecy with main point and sub-points: _____

_____

_____

_____

_____

_____

_____

_____

_____

_____

_____

_____

_____

_____

_____

_____

_____

_____

_____

_____

_____

_____

_____

_____

_____

_____

_____

_____

_____

_____

_____

_____

_____

_____

_____

_____

_____

_____

The Organic Shepherding
of the Pneumatic Christ

Scripture Reading: Psa. 23; John 21:15-17; Heb. 13:20-21; 1 Pet. 2:25; 5:1-4

Day 1

I. **In Psalm 22 Christ was the Redeemer and the Regenerator, in Psalm 23 He is now the Shepherd, and in Psalm 24 He will be the King who will regain the entire earth through the church, His Body, the people whom He has redeemed and regenerated and is shepherding today:**

A. In His heavenly ministry Christ is shepherding people, and we need to cooperate with Him by shepherding people; this is the apostolic ministry in cooperation with Christ's heavenly ministry (John 21:15-17; Heb. 13:20; 1 Pet. 5:1-4).

B. If all the churches receive the teaching to participate in Christ's wonderful shepherding, there will be a big revival in the recovery; our cooperation with Him in His heavenly ministry of shepherding will build up His Body, prepare His bride, for His second coming to be the King in the next age.

C. To shepherd people is to cherish and nourish them, as illustrated by the entire New Testament:

   1. Christ as the Son of Man came to redeem us from sin (1 Tim. 1:15)—cherishing.

   2. Christ as the Son of God came to impart the divine life into us abundantly (John 10:10b)—nourishing.

Day 2

II. **The all-inclusive Christ is our inward, pneumatic Shepherd, taking care of our inner being (v. 11; Heb. 13:20-21; 1 Pet. 5:1-4; 2:25).**

III. **The indwelling, pneumatic Christ is "my Shepherd," and under His all-inclusive, tender care "I will lack nothing" (2 Cor. 3:17a; 2 Tim. 4:22; 1 Cor. 6:17; Phil. 1:19; Psa. 23:1).**

IV. **According to Psalm 23, Christ shepherds us in five stages:**

A. The initial stage is the enjoyment of Christ as the green pastures and of the Spirit as the waters of rest (v. 2).

B. The second stage is the revival and transformation on the paths of righteousness (v. 3).

C. The third stage is the experience of the resurrected pneumatic Christ while walking through the valley of the shadow of death (v. 4).

D. The fourth stage is the deeper and higher enjoyment of the resurrected Christ in fighting against the adversaries (v. 5).

E. The fifth stage is the lifelong enjoyment of the divine goodness and lovingkindness in the house of Jehovah (v. 6).

V. **In His organic shepherding, the pneumatic Christ "makes me lie down in green pastures" (v. 2a):**

A. *Green* signifies the riches of life; the green pastures are Christ Himself as our nourishment (John 10:9).

B. Christ can be our green pasture, our feeding place, through His incarnation, death, and resurrection.

C. The base of the Greek word for *economy* in 1 Timothy 1:4 is of the same origin as that for *pasture* in John 10:9, implying a distribution of pasture to the flock; this reveals that Psalm 23 is a psalm on God's economy, His household administration, to dispense Himself as the green pastures into His people and build them up to be the house of Jehovah, the divine-human incorporation of the processed and consummated Triune God with His redeemed, regenerated, transformed, and glorified tripartite people (v. 6).

Day 3 VI. **In His organic shepherding, the pneumatic Christ "leads me beside waters of rest" (v. 2b):**

A. The waters of rest signify the Spirit, the consummated Spirit after Christ's resurrection (John 7:37-39).

B. Both the green pastures and the restful waters are the resurrected, pneumatic Christ as the life-giving Spirit (1 Cor. 15:45b; John 14:16-18).

VII. **In His organic shepherding, the pneumatic Christ "restores my soul" (Psa. 23:3a):**

A. For our soul to be restored means that we are revived; restoring also includes renewing and transforming (Rom. 12:2; 2 Cor. 3:18).

B. Our Lord, as the Shepherd and Overseer of our souls, shepherds us by caring for the welfare of our inner being and by exercising His oversight over the condition of our real person (1 Pet. 2:25):

1. Christ takes care of us in a tender, all-inclusive way; this kind of shepherding is an inward, intrinsic, organic comforting (John 14:16, 26; cf. 2 Cor. 1:3-4).

2. Because our soul is very complicated, we need Christ, who is the life-giving Spirit in our spirit, to shepherd us in our soul, to take care of our mind, emotion, and will and of our problems, needs, and wounds (cf. Isa. 61:1).

VIII. **In His organic shepherding, the pneumatic Christ "guides me on the paths of righteousness / For His name's sake" (Psa. 23:3b):**

A. Christ guides us (to walk according to the spirit) on the paths of righteousness (to fulfill the requirement of righteousness—Rom. 8:4).

B. *The paths of righteousness* indicates our walk (v. 4; Gal. 5:16, 25).

C. *For His name's sake* means for the sake of His person, His living person as the pneumatic Christ (Matt. 28:19; 18:20; Col. 3:17).

D. Christ restores our soul so that we may take His way and walk on the paths of righteousness:

1. We need to be proper and balanced in our mind, emotion, and will; otherwise, we cannot be righteous.

2. Under the organic shepherding of the pneumatic Christ, we are balanced, corrected, and adjusted.

3. In all that we do, we need to be under Christ's shepherding, taking Christ as both our paths and our righteousness.

E. Righteousness is being right with persons, things, and matters before God according to His righteous and strict requirements (Matt. 5:20).

F. Righteousness is a matter of God's kingdom; thus, righteousness issues from God for His administration and is related to His government and rule (6:33; Psa. 89:14a; 97:2b; Isa. 32:1).

G. Righteousness is the living out and genuine expression of Christ, who as the life-giving Spirit lives in us (Rev. 19:8; 2 Cor. 3:9).

Day 4 IX. **Under the organic shepherding of the pneumatic Christ, "even though I walk / Through the valley of the shadow of death, / I do not fear evil, / For You are with me; / Your rod and Your staff, / They comfort me" (Psa. 23:4):**

A. For the pneumatic Christ to be with us means that we enjoy His invisible presence, which is special, personal, and intimate (Matt. 28:20b; 2 Tim. 4:22a).

B. The presence of the pneumatic Christ is a comfort, a rescue, and a sustaining power to us when we are walking through the valley of the shadow of death.

C. When we are in the valley, we should simply remain there and rest in the Lord; our resting in the Lord will shorten the valley, reduce the shadow, and remove the death.

D. The Lord's rod, a symbol of His authority, is for our protection:

  1. We are under the Lord's authority and take the way marked out by Him.

  2. Every negative thing—death, darkness, fear, evil—is under His rule, control, and authority.

E. The Lord's staff is for guidance, instruction, training, direction, and sustenance.

F. Under the organic shepherding of the pneumatic Christ in the valley of the shadow of death, we experience God as the God of resurrection and may attain to the out-resurrection (John 11:25; 2 Cor. 1:8-9; Phil. 3:10-11).

Day 5   **X.** **Under the organic shepherding of the pneumatic Christ, He spreads "a table before me / In the presence of my adversaries; / You anoint my head with oil; / My cup runs over" (Psa. 23:5):**

   A. The Lord spreads a table before us in the presence of our adversaries (v. 5a; cf. 2 Sam. 4:4; 9:7, 13; Gen. 14:18-20; Neh. 4:17).

   B. The Lord anoints our head with oil (as at a festal banquet), and our cup (the cup of blessing) runs over (Psa. 23:5b; Heb. 1:9; 1 Cor. 10:16a, 21).

   C. In Psalm 23:5 we have the Triune God—the Son as the table, the feast, the Spirit as the anointing oil, and the Father as the source of blessing.

Day 6   **XI.** **Under the organic shepherding of the pneumatic Christ, "surely goodness and lovingkindness will follow me / All the days of my life, / And I will dwell in the house of Jehovah / For the length of my days" (v. 6):**

   A. *Goodness* refers to the grace of Christ, *lovingkindness* refers to the love of the Father, and *follow* refers to the fellowship of the Spirit; thus, the grace of the Son, the love of the Father, and the fellowship of the Spirit are with us (2 Cor. 13:14).

   B. The enjoyment of the processed and consummated Triune God ushers us into the enjoyment of God in the house of God (Christ, the church, and the New Jerusalem—John 1:14; 2:21; 1 Tim. 3:15-16; Eph. 2:22; Rev. 21:2-3, 22) for the length of our days (in the present age, in the coming age, and in eternity).

   C. We need to seek to dwell in the house of God all the days of our life (Psa. 27:4-8):

      1. To behold the beauty (loveliness, pleasantness, delightfulness) of God (vv. 4, 8; 2 Cor. 3:18).

      2. To inquire of God, checking with God about everything in our daily life (Psa. 27:4b; cf. Josh. 9:14).

      3. To be concealed in God's shelter and to hide ourselves in the hiding place of God's tent (Psa. 27:5; 31:20).

4. To be raised up and have our head lifted up by God (27:5b-6a).

5. To offer sacrifices of shouts of joy with singing and psalming to God for the glory of God (v. 6b; Heb. 13:15; Phil. 2:11).

XII. **Psalm 23 is the link between Psalms 22 and 24; it is by Christ's wonderful shepherding and by our entering into this shepherding (the intrinsic significance of the vital groups) that the Body of Christ will be built up with His redeemed and regenerated ones and that the bride will be prepared for Him to return as the King in the next age in the manifestation of His kingdom.**

Morning Nourishment

John He said to him again a second time, Simon, *son* of
21:16 John, do you love Me?...Shepherd My sheep.
1 Pet. For you were like sheep being led astray, but you
 2:25 have now returned to the Shepherd and Overseer of
      your souls.
5:2,4 Shepherd the flock of God among you...And when
      the Chief Shepherd is manifested, you will receive the
      unfading crown of glory.

John 21 reveals the apostolic ministry in cooperation with
Christ's heavenly ministry. After Christ ascended to the heavens,
He began His heavenly ministry. In doing this He raised up a group
of His followers as His apostles who could fully cooperate with
Him....What He was doing in the heavens, the apostles did on
earth to carry out His heavenly ministry....Christ's heavenly ministry and the apostles' ministry on the earth cooperate together to
carry out God's New Testament economy.

The Lord's shepherding was firstly in His earthly ministry
(Matt. 9:36). The Lord saw the Israelites as sheep harassed by
their leaders; they were cast away like sheep not having a shepherd. The Lord as the Shepherd of God's elect prayed, and God
told His sent One to appoint twelve apostles that they might take
care of the sheep of God (Matt. 10:1-6).

The Lord's shepherding is secondly in His heavenly ministry
(1 Pet. 5:4) to take care of the church of God, issuing in His Body.
When He was on the earth, He was shepherding. After His resurrection and ascension to the heavens, He is still shepherding.
(*Crystallization-study of the Gospel of John*, pp. 130-131)

Today's Reading

When the Lord stayed with His disciples after His resurrection and before His ascension, in one of His appearings, He commissioned Peter to feed His lambs and shepherd His sheep in His
absence, while He is in the heavens (John 21:15-17). Shepherding
implies feeding, but it includes much more than feeding. To shepherd is to take all-inclusive tender care of the flock.

This is to incorporate the apostolic ministry with Christ's heavenly ministry to take care of God's flock.

Peter was so impressed with this commission of the Lord that in his first book he told the believers that they were like sheep being led astray, but they had now returned to the Shepherd and Overseer (Christ) of their souls (1 Pet. 2:25). Christ's shepherding of His flock includes His caring for their outward things and also their inner being, their souls....Christ indwells us to be our life and everything, but He is also overseeing, observing, the condition and situation of our inner being...by exercising His oversight over the condition of our soul, our real person.

The main purpose and goal of the apostolic ministry incorporated with Christ's heavenly ministry are to build up the Body of Christ which will consummate the New Jerusalem for the accomplishment of the eternal economy of God. (*Crystallization-study of the Gospel of John,* pp. 131-133)

If all the churches receive this teaching to participate in Christ's wonderful shepherding, there will be a big revival in the recovery. In the past we did much speaking and teaching with very little shepherding. Shepherding and teaching should be like two feet for our move with the Lord. Our shepherding should always be with teaching, and our teaching should always be with shepherding.

John 21...reveals the apostolic ministry in cooperation with Christ's heavenly ministry. In His heavenly ministry Christ is shepherding people, and we need to cooperate with Him by shepherding people. Without shepherding, our work for the Lord cannot be effective. We must learn all the truths so that we may have something to speak and go to contact people to shepherd them.

Christ as the Son of Man came to redeem us from sin (1 Tim. 1:15)—cherishing. This is the first part of the New Testament.... Christ as the Son of God came to impart the divine life into us abundantly (John 10:10)—nourishing. This is the second part of the New Testament. (*The Vital Groups,* pp. 40, 87)

Further Reading: Crystallization-study of the Gospel of John, msg. 13

Enlightenment and inspiration: _____

_____
_____
_____

Morning Nourishment

Psa. Jehovah is my Shepherd; I will lack nothing. He
23:1-2 makes me <u>lie down in green pastures</u>; <u>He leads me</u>
<u>beside waters of rest</u>.

John I am the door; if anyone enters through Me, he
10:9 shall be saved and shall go in and go out and shall
find pasture.

11 I am the good Shepherd; the good Shepherd lays
down His life for the sheep.

Psalm 23 is full of the enjoyment of Christ as our Shepherd....Christ as the Shepherd leads us through five stages of enjoyment. The first stage is that of the green pastures and the waters of rest (v. 2). The second stage is the paths of righteousness (v. 3), and the third stage is the experience of Christ's presence through the valley of the shadow of death (v. 4). The fourth stage is the deeper and higher enjoyment of the resurrected Christ, in which we enjoy the Lord's table in the presence of our adversaries (v. 5). This implies that we are enjoying the Lord on the battlefield. The fifth and final stage is the lifelong enjoyment of the divine goodness and lovingkindness in the house of Jehovah (v. 6). Psalm 24 goes on to show that the victorious Christ as the King of glory is coming to reign as the King in God's kingdom. All these points in the Psalms indicate that Christ is enjoyable. (*Life-study of the Psalms*, p. 153)

Today's Reading

[Psalm 23] tells us that Christ's shepherding of us is in five stages....I would like us to consider what stage we are in among these five stages of Christ's shepherding. The first stage is the initial stage of enjoyment. This is just like elementary school. In our educational system there are five stages—elementary, junior high, high school, college, and graduate school. This is comparable to the five stages of Christ's shepherding in Psalm 23. Many of us are in "elementary school" while others are in "high school" in their experience of Christ.

The resurrected Christ shepherds us first in the initial stage of enjoyment in green pastures and at waters of rest (Psa. 23:1-2). Because He is our Shepherd, we will lack nothing (Phil. 1:19b). Right after we were saved, we entered into this first stage of enjoyment. In John 21 the Lord Jesus asked Peter if he loved Him. When Peter said that he did love the Lord, the Lord charged him to feed His lambs (v. 15). We need to be like nursing mothers to cherish and feed the little ones under our care (1 Thes. 2:7). Right after a child is delivered, a mother feeds the child so he can grow.

In the initial stage of the enjoyment of Christ, the lambs, the infants, feed on Christ as the green pasture (John 10:9). Infants do not have table manners. All the little lambs lie down to eat the pasture without any thought of manners. Christ makes us to lie down, not sit down in a mannerly way, in green pastures. This kind of eating, without the thought for proper manners, is more enjoyable.

Psalm 23:2 says, "He makes me lie down in green pastures." The color green signifies the riches of life. When we see the green trees and pastures, we see the riches of life. If the trees are yellow and dried up and the grass is brown, this indicates death.

The green pastures signify the Lord Jesus. The Lord Jesus spoke concerning this in John 10. He said that His sheep would hear His voice and follow Him out of the fold to enjoy the green pastures as the flock (vv. 9, 16). In John 10, Christ is the door (v. 9), the Shepherd (v. 11), and the pasture (v. 9). Christ Himself is our pasture, our nourishment. He is the feeding place for all the sheep. In John 6 Christ said that He is the bread of life (v. 35) to nourish us (v. 57). The "bread" for the sheep is the green pasture, so the green pasture is Christ. Christ can be our green pasture through His incarnation, death, and resurrection. After His incarnation, death, and resurrection, He is growing here as the green pasture for our nourishment. (*Life-study of the Psalms,* pp. 139-140, 138)

Further Reading: The Vital Groups, msgs. 4, 6, 9

Enlightenment and inspiration: _____

_____

_____

_____

Morning Nourishment

Psa. ...He leads me beside waters of rest. He restores my
23:2-3 soul; He guides me on the paths of righteousness for
His name's sake.
John He who believes into Me...out of his innermost being
7:38-39 shall flow rivers of living water. But this He said concerning the Spirit...

He also leads us to waters of rest (Psa. 23:2b; 1 Cor. 12:13b).
The green pastures are Christ, and the waters of rest are the
Spirit. The Spirit is the restful waters. When we go to take care of
the new ones, we must not only feed them with Christ but also
help them to drink of the Spirit. We must help them to call on the
name of the Lord and to pray. This is to help them to drink the
Spirit by exercising their spirit.

The waters we drink are very restful. If someone served us food
without anything to drink, this would not be so pleasant or rest-
ful. We would not have a comfortable feeling. This is why we need
Christ as the pasture and the Spirit as the waters of rest....In one
aspect, He is our pasture, our food, to feed us. In another aspect,
He is the life-giving Spirit as waters to bring us the proper rest.
Both the pastures and the waters are the resurrected pneumatic
Christ as the life-giving Spirit. (*Life-study of the Psalms*, p. 141)

Today's Reading

Psalm 23:3 says, "He restores my soul; / He guides me on the paths
of righteousness / For His name's sake." This is the second stage....To
restore our soul is to revive us. Restoring also includes renewing and
transforming. This corresponds with the New Testament teaching in Romans 12:2 which says that we need to be transformed by
the renewing of the mind,...the leading part of our soul.

[Christ] restores us—revives and transforms us—in our soul
to make us take His way, to walk on the paths of righteousness.
Both the paths and righteousness are Christ. The resurrected
Christ today is our paths. In order to be a proper sister or a proper
brother, we need Christ as our paths, as our way. A sister who does
not behave and walk as a female does not have Christ as her

paths. A brother who acts foolishly does not have Christ as his paths. Some brothers need a particular path to be an elder. Others need a path to be a co-worker. We also need a path to act as Christians and another path to work in God's economy. We need many paths, the paths of righteousness, in our Christian life and work.

John 7 says that when we drink of the life-giving Spirit as the living water, we will flow out, not just one river but many rivers (v. 38). There is a river of the proper humanity, a river of kindness, a river of love, a river of patience, etc. We need many rivers. In the same way, we need a path of humility, a path of loving, a path of patience, etc. These are the paths of righteousness.

Righteousness is to be right with people before God according to His righteous and strict requirements. We...[all] are short of the paths to be right. We have to take the paths of righteousness by being restored—revived and transformed—in our soul, which comprises our mind, our emotion, and our will. We must be proper and balanced in our mind, our emotion, and our will. Otherwise, we cannot be righteous; we cannot be right with man and with God.

A shepherd has a staff to guide and instruct the sheep....We all have to be under the Lord's shepherding in all that we do. His shepherding is a kind of balancing, correcting, and adjusting.

He guides us (to walk according to the spirit) on the paths of righteousness (to fulfill the requirement of righteousness—Rom. 8:4). Righteousness can be fulfilled only by those who walk according to their spirit. We have three parts—body, soul, and spirit (1 Thes. 5:23). We should not do things according to our body, because it is full of lusts. We should not do things according to our soul, because it is full of opinions. Instead, we should do things according to our spirit. When we walk according to the spirit, we fulfill the righteous requirement of the law. Christ as our Shepherd leads us in the paths of righteousness for His name's sake—in the person of the resurrected pneumatic Christ. (*Life-study of the Psalms,* pp. 141-143)

Further Reading: Life-study of the Psalms, msg. 11

Enlightenment and inspiration: _____

_____

_____

_____

Morning Nourishment

Psa. Even though I walk through the valley of the shadow
23:4 of death, I do not fear evil, for You are with me; Your
rod and Your staff, they comfort me.
2 Tim. The Lord be with your spirit. Grace be with you.
4:22

The third stage is the stage of the experience of the presence of
the resurrected pneumatic Christ through the valley of the shadow
of death (Psa. 23:4). Even though we walk through the valley of
the shadow of death, we do not fear evil, for the pneumatic Christ
is with us (2 Tim. 4:22). This means that we experience His presence. For Him to be with us is for us to enjoy His presence. His
presence is a comfort, a rescue, and a sustaining power to us when
we are walking in the valley of the shadow of death. (*Life-study of
the Psalms*, p. 144)

Today's Reading

We human beings cannot avoid having troubles as we live on
this earth. A husband's wife who takes care of him and the children may suddenly become so ill that she is unable to walk. Then
this brother gets into the valley, which is under a shadow and full
of death. Some saints may have children who are crippled. This
brings these saints into the valley. A brother may be an elder in a
locality, and the Lord may suddenly bring in another elder, with
whom it is difficult for this brother to coordinate. This other elder
then becomes the valley of the shadow of death to the first elder.

When we are in the valley, the best way for us to deal with it is
to rest. The tests in the valley always tempt us to do something so
that we can come out of the valley. But the more we do, the more
the valley extends. We just need to be quiet, to rest.

Our resting in the Lord will shorten the valley, reduce the
shadow, and remove the death. We should not talk about our
being in the valley. The more we talk, the wider the valley
becomes. The best way is for us to forget that we are in the valley,
because we have the Lord with us. We do not fear evil, because He
is with us. Second Timothy 4:22 says that the Lord is with our
spirit. The Lord is not merely within us in a general way, but He is

in our spirit in a particular way. If we have had the proper experience in the valley, we can testify that it was a place for us to enjoy the Lord's presence in such a close way.

In 1943 there was a big revival in the church in Chefoo, my hometown in mainland China. At that time we were under the invasion of the Japanese army. They were wondering how I could draw so many people. They studied me secretly for a few months, and then in May of 1943, they came to get me. They brought me to their military police headquarters, and I was put into prison for thirty days. That was a real valley to me....I could have been killed by them at any time. I was under their threatening and torture for two three-hour sessions a day.

One day they purposely decided not to give me any food. One of them came to me and, not being able to speak Chinese, he pointed up to the heavens, indicating that I should ask my God to give me food.... [Another prisoner], however, insisted on sharing his food with me.

One day when I was alone, as I was praying, I had a deep sense that the Lord was there with me in a special, intimate way. I was in the valley, and the Lord caused me not to fear any evil. Eventually, I was preserved and protected by the Lord from being harmed. After thirty days, the Japanese released me. That was a real experience and enjoyment of the Lord's presence in the deep valley of the shadow of death.

In the valley of the shadow of death, the Lord's rod and His staff—His protection, His guidance, and His sustenance—comfort us. The rod is for protection. If a wolf comes, the shepherd uses his rod to protect the flock. The staff is for training, for direction, for guidance, and also for sustenance. The Lord has the rod to protect us, and He has the staff to train us, to instruct us, to guide us, and to sustain us. We experience the Lord's protection and guiding in the valley of the shadow of death. (*Life-study of the Psalms,* pp. 144-146)

Further Reading: Life-study of the Psalms, msg. 11

Enlightenment and inspiration: _____

_____

_____

_____

Morning Nourishment

Psa. You spread a table before me in the presence of my
23:5 adversaries; You anoint my head with oil; my cup
runs over.

133:2 It is like the fine oil upon the head that ran down
upon the beard, upon Aaron's beard, that ran down
upon the hem of his garments.

1 Cor. The cup of blessing which we bless, is it not the fel-
10:16 lowship of the blood of Christ?...

Now we come to the fourth stage of the deeper and higher
enjoyment of the resurrected Christ (Psa. 23:5). The Lord spreads a
table—a feast—before us in the presence of our adversaries (1 Cor.
10:21). The Lord's table is a feast. Every Lord's Day when we come
to His table to take the feast, it is always in the presence of our
adversaries. Every day is a fighting day to us. We Christians have
to fight. Otherwise, we will be defeated. There may be adversaries
in our business, in our home, and even in the church. On the one
hand, we enjoy the feast of the Lord, and on the other hand, we
should fight for the victory. If we are defeated during the week, it
will be difficult for us to enjoy the Lord's table that much. We need
to fight the battle in the Lord all week long before we come to the
Lord's table. Then we will be able to have a rich enjoyment of the
Lord as our feast at His table. (*Life-study of the Psalms,* p. 146)

Today's Reading

In the fourth stage of the deeper and higher enjoyment of the
resurrected Christ, the Lord anoints our head with oil (of exultant
joy—Heb. 1:9); our cup (of blessing—1 Cor. 10:16a) runs over. To
anoint the head is to anoint the whole body. Psalm 133 speaks of
the ointment upon the head spreading down to the skirts of the
garments. No doubt, this is the anointing of the compound, life-
giving Spirit in Christ's resurrection. All the riches of Christ's
being and doing are compounded together in this anointing compound ointment.

The Bible uses the word *cup* to indicate blessing. The cup of
blessing runs over. Psalm 23:5 speaks of the table, the feast, which

is Christ with His riches for our enjoyment. Then there is the anointing oil, which is the Spirit. Then there is the cup of blessing, which refers to the Father. The Father is the blessing, even the source of blessing. Thus, in verse five there is the Triune God— the Son as the feast, the Spirit as the anointing oil, and the Father as the source of blessing. (*Life-study of the Psalms,* pp. 146-147)

After the valley you may think that everything should be so wonderful. But the next station is the battlefield. It is after the valley of the shadow of death that you are qualified and equipped for fighting. Allow me to say that however living and active you are now, I can have no trust in you. You need to pass the test; you need to pass through the valley of the shadow of death. The potters, after making certain objects of clay, place them in an oven to be burnt. There is a great difference between vessels of clay which have been burnt and those which have not. The valley of the shadow of death is the place for us to be burnt. After this experience we are qualified and equipped to fight the battle.

But on the battlefield, praise the Lord, there is a table set before us. "You spread a table before me / In the presence of my adversaries" (v. 5). The fighting on the battlefield is the feasting. While we are fighting, we are feasting. We may tell the enemy, "Send your armies; all your armies will be the courses of our feast." The Old Testament tells us that even the enemies are our food (Num. 14:9). For us Christians, the enemies are the best food. This is a table, a table spread with many courses. And this is not all. It is here on the battlefield that we experience the anointing of our head with oil and our cup running over. It is really so. In our experiences, the more we are on the battlefield fighting for the Lord, the more we sense that we are under the anointing, that we are feasting, and that our cup is running over. It is really good. But still this is not all. (*Christ and the Church Revealed and Typified in the Psalms,* p. 54)

Further Reading: Christ and the Church Revealed and Typified in the Psalms, ch. 5

Enlightenment and inspiration: _____

_____

_____

_____

Morning Nourishment

Psa. **Surely goodness and lovingkindness will follow me**
23:6 **all the days of my life, and I will dwell in the house of**
Jehovah for the length of *my* days.
27:4 **One thing I have asked from Jehovah; that do I seek:**
to dwell in the house of Jehovah all the days of my
life, to behold the beauty of Jehovah, and to inquire in
His temple.

Psalm 23:6 speaks of the fifth stage of the lifelong enjoyment of the divine goodness and lovingkindness in the house of Jehovah. Surely goodness and lovingkindness will follow us (the grace of Christ and the love of God will be with us—2 Cor. 13:14) all the days of our life (in the present age). *Goodness* refers to the grace of Christ, *lovingkindness* refers to the love of the Father, and *follow* refers to the fellowship of the Spirit. Second Corinthians 13:14 reveals the move of the Triune God for us to enjoy all His riches. The grace of the Son, the love of the Father, and the fellowship of the Spirit are with us. This is the fifth stage of our enjoyment of the Triune God in Psalm 23. (*Life-study of the Psalms,* p. 147)

Today's Reading

Eventually, this enjoyment will usher us into the house of God. We will dwell in the house of Jehovah (the church and the New Jerusalem—1 Tim. 3:15-16; Rev. 21:2-3, 22) for the length of our days (in the present age and in the coming age and in eternity).... Today we are in the church. If we are overcomers, we will be in the kingdom of one thousand years in the New Jerusalem. Eventually, in eternity we will be in the New Jerusalem with all of the chosen and redeemed saints. God's house is our dwelling place where we enjoy the Triune God—the Son's grace, the Father's love, and the Spirit's fellowship. Today we enjoy the Triune God in the church, and in the future we will enjoy Him in the New Jerusalem.

If we are not in the church, we lose the shepherding of Christ. ...This is because He is the Shepherd of the flock, and the flock is the church. To get out of the church is to get out of the flock, and the Shepherd is always with the flock.

David said that he sought to dwell in the house of God all the days of his life (Psa. 27:4-6)....In verse 4 David said that he desired to behold the beauty of Jehovah in His house. The Hebrew word for *beauty* implies loveliness, pleasantness, and delightfulness. When we are beholding God's beauty, we are in a very pleasant atmosphere. Second Corinthians 3:18 says that we can have an unveiled face to behold the glorious face of the Lord in glory. In our time with the Lord in the morning, it is best to have short prayers with a number of "selahs" so that we can behold the Lord, look at the Lord.

The psalmist also inquired of God in His temple (Psa. 27:4b). This means that we can check with God about everything in our daily life.

In Psalm 27:5 David said, "For He will conceal me in His shelter / In the day of trouble; [/ He will hide me in the hiding place of His tent]."...When evils, calamities, are taking place, we can be concealed in God's shelter, and the evils cannot "see" us, cannot affect us. When someone is trying to capture us, there is a hiding place in God's tent where no one can find us. To be concealed is for getting away from the damage of calamities. To hide is for getting away from the ones who want to get us. The house of God is both a shelter and a hiding place.

David also said that God would raise him up upon a rock and that he would have his head lifted up by God (27:5c, 6a). Most of the time, we drop our heads. We do not have our heads lifted up.... We are earthly people, always looking upon the earth. It seems that we have lost something valuable and that we are looking on the ground for it. But when Abraham heard God's promise in the night, God told him to look toward heaven at the stars. Then God told Abraham that his descendants would be as numerous as the stars (Gen. 15:5). We need to forget about all of the earthly things. Instead, we need to look up. We need to lift up our heads and say, "Praise the Lord! Hallelujah!" This is a glory to Him. (*Life-study of the Psalms,* pp. 147-148, 160-161)

Further Reading: Life-study of the Psalms, msg. 12

Enlightenment and inspiration: _____

_____

_____

_____

Hymns, #1170

1   The Lord is my Shepherd forever,
     He maketh me down to lie,
   He leads me beside the still waters
     O how He does satisfy!

     Surely goodness and mercy shall follow me
       All the days, all the days of my life;
     Surely goodness and mercy shall follow me
       All the days, all the days of my life.
     And I shall dwell in the house of the Lord forever,
       And I shall feast at the table spread for me;
     Surely goodness and mercy shall follow me
       All the days, all the days of my life.

2   My Shepherd Himself is my pasture,
     My Shepherd, the waters of rest;
   I eat of His riches in spirit,
     I drink, and O how I am blest!

3   My Shepherd my soul is restoring,
     My will, and emotion, and mind;
   And though through the valley I'm walking,
     O what a Companion I find!

4   A table prepared by my Shepherd
     I feast on and Satan destroy;
   My head is anointed with oil,
     My cup runneth over with joy!

5   And now in His house I am dwelling
     Enjoying the goodness of God;
   My pleasure is far beyond telling,
     My pleasure is Jesus my Lord!

Composition for prophecy with main point and sub-points: _____

_____
_____
_____
_____
_____
_____
_____
_____
_____
_____
_____
_____
_____
_____
_____
_____
_____
_____
_____
_____
_____
_____
_____
_____
_____
_____
_____
_____
_____
_____
_____
_____
_____
_____
_____
_____

Reading Schedule for the Recovery Version of the Old Testament with Footnotes

Wk.	Lord's Day	Monday	Tuesday	Wednesday	Thursday	Friday	Saturday
1	☐ Gen 1:1-5	☐ 1:6-23	☐ 1:24-31	☐ 2:1-9	☐ 2:10-25	☐ 3:1-13	☐ 3:14-24
2	☐ 4:1-26	☐ 5:1-32	☐ 6:1-22	☐ 7:1—8:3	☐ 8:4-22	☐ 9:1-29	☐ 10:1-32
3	☐ 11:1-32	☐ 12:1-20	☐ 13:1-18	☐ 14:1-24	☐ 15:1-21	☐ 16:1-16	☐ 17:1-27
4	☐ 18:1-33	☐ 19:1-38	☐ 20:1-18	☐ 21:1-34	☐ 22:1-24	☐ 23:1—24:27	☐ 24:28-67
5	☐ 25:1-34	☐ 26:1-35	☐ 27:1-46	☐ 28:1-22	☐ 29:1-35	☐ 30:1-43	☐ 31:1-55
6	☐ 32:1-32	☐ 33:1—34:31	☐ 35:1-29	☐ 36:1-43	☐ 37:1-36	☐ 38:1—39:23	☐ 40:1—41:13
7	☐ 41:14-57	☐ 42:1-38	☐ 43:1-34	☐ 44:1-34	☐ 45:1-28	☐ 46:1-34	☐ 47:1-31
8	☐ 48:1-22	☐ 49:1-15	☐ 49:16-33	☐ 50:1-26	☐ Exo 1:1-22	☐ 2:1-25	☐ 3:1-22
9	☐ 4:1-31	☐ 5:1-23	☐ 6:1-30	☐ 7:1-25	☐ 8:1-32	☐ 9:1-35	☐ 10:1-29
10	☐ 11:1-10	☐ 12:1-14	☐ 12:15-36	☐ 12:37-51	☐ 13:1-22	☐ 14:1-31	☐ 15:1-27
11	☐ 16:1-36	☐ 17:1-16	☐ 18:1-27	☐ 19:1-25	☐ 20:1-26	☐ 21:1-36	☐ 22:1-31
12	☐ 23:1-33	☐ 24:1-18	☐ 25:1-22	☐ 25:23-40	☐ 26:1-14	☐ 26:15-37	☐ 27:1-21
13	☐ 28:1-21	☐ 28:22-43	☐ 29:1-21	☐ 29:22-46	☐ 30:1-10	☐ 30:11-38	☐ 31:1-17
14	☐ 31:18—32:35	☐ 33:1-23	☐ 34:1-35	☐ 35:1-35	☐ 36:1-38	☐ 37:1-29	☐ 38:1-31
15	☐ 39:1-43	☐ 40:1-38	☐ Lev 1:1-17	☐ 2:1-16	☐ 3:1-17	☐ 4:1-35	☐ 5:1-19
16	☐ 6:1-30	☐ 7:1-38	☐ 8:1-36	☐ 9:1-24	☐ 10:1-20	☐ 11:1-47	☐ 12:1-8
17	☐ 13:1-28	☐ 13:29-59	☐ 14:1-18	☐ 14:19-32	☐ 14:33-57	☐ 15:1-33	☐ 16:1-17
18	☐ 16:18-34	☐ 17:1-16	☐ 18:1-30	☐ 19:1-37	☐ 20:1-27	☐ 21:1-24	☐ 22:1-33
19	☐ 23:1-22	☐ 23:23-44	☐ 24:1-23	☐ 25:1-23	☐ 25:24-55	☐ 26:1-24	☐ 26:25-46
20	☐ 27:1-34	☐ Num 1:1-54	☐ 2:1-34	☐ 3:1-51	☐ 4:1-49	☐ 5:1-31	☐ 6:1-27
21	☐ 7:1-41	☐ 7:42-88	☐ 7:89—8:26	☐ 9:1-23	☐ 10:1-36	☐ 11:1-35	☐ 12:1—13:33
22	☐ 14:1-45	☐ 15:1-41	☐ 16:1-50	☐ 17:1—18:7	☐ 18:8-32	☐ 19:1-22	☐ 20:1-29
23	☐ 21:1-35	☐ 22:1-41	☐ 23:1-30	☐ 24:1-25	☐ 25:1-18	☐ 26:1-65	☐ 27:1-23
24	☐ 28:1-31	☐ 29:1-40	☐ 30:1—31:24	☐ 31:25-54	☐ 32:1-42	☐ 33:1-56	☐ 34:1-29
25	☐ 35:1-34	☐ 36:1-13	☐ Deut 1:1-46	☐ 2:1-37	☐ 3:1-29	☐ 4:1-49	☐ 5:1-33
26	☐ 6:1—7:26	☐ 8:1-20	☐ 9:1-29	☐ 10:1-22	☐ 11:1-32	☐ 12:1-32	☐ 13:1—14:21

Reading Schedule for the Recovery Version of the Old Testament with Footnotes

Wk.	Lord's Day	Monday	Tuesday	Wednesday	Thursday	Friday	Saturday
27	☐ 14:22—15:23	☐ 16:1-22	☐ 17:1—18:8	☐ 18:9—19:21	☐ 20:1—21:17	☐ 21:18—22:30	☐ 23:1-25
28	☐ 24:1-22	☐ 25:1-19	☐ 26:1-19	☐ 27:1-26	☐ 28:1-68	☐ 29:1-29	☐ 30:1—31:29
29	☐ 31:30—32:52	☐ 33:1-29	☐ 34:1-12	☐ Josh 1:1-18	☐ 2:1-24	☐ 3:1-17	☐ 4:1-24
30	☐ 5:1-15	☐ 6:1-27	☐ 7:1-26	☐ 8:1-35	☐ 9:1-27	☐ 10:1-43	☐ 11:1—12:24
31	☐ 13:1-33	☐ 14:1—15:63	☐ 16:1—18:28	☐ 19:1-51	☐ 20:1—21:45	☐ 22:1-34	☐ 23:1—24:33
32	☐ Judg 1:1-36	☐ 2:1-23	☐ 3:1-31	☐ 4:1-24	☐ 5:1-31	☐ 6:1-40	☐ 7:1-25
33	☐ 8:1-35	☐ 9:1-57	☐ 10:1—11:40	☐ 12:1—13:25	☐ 14:1—15:20	☐ 16:1-31	☐ 17:1—18:31
34	☐ 19:1-30	☐ 20:1-48	☐ 21:1-25	☐ Ruth 1:1-22	☐ 2:1-23	☐ 3:1-18	☐ 4:1-22
35	☐ 1 Sam 1:1-28	☐ 2:1-36	☐ 3:1—4:22	☐ 5:1—6:21	☐ 7:1—8:22	☐ 9:1-27	☐ 10:1—11:15
36	☐ 12:1—13:23	☐ 14:1-52	☐ 15:1-35	☐ 16:1-23	☐ 17:1-58	☐ 18:1-30	☐ 19:1-24
37	☐ 20:1-42	☐ 21:1—22:23	☐ 23:1—24:22	☐ 25:1-44	☐ 26:1-25	☐ 27:1—28:25	☐ 29:1—30:31
38	☐ 31:1-13	☐ 2 Sam 1:1-27	☐ 2:1-32	☐ 3:1-39	☐ 4:1—5:25	☐ 6:1-23	☐ 7:1-29
39	☐ 8:1—9:13	☐ 10:1—11:27	☐ 12:1-31	☐ 13:1-39	☐ 14:1-33	☐ 15:1—16:23	☐ 17:1—18:33
40	☐ 19:1-43	☐ 20:1—21:22	☐ 22:1-51	☐ 23:1-39	☐ 24:1-25	☐ 1 Kings 1:1-19	☐ 1:20-53
41	☐ 2:1-46	☐ 3:1-28	☐ 4:1-34	☐ 5:1—6:38	☐ 7:1-22	☐ 7:23-51	☐ 8:1-36
42	☐ 8:37-66	☐ 9:1-28	☐ 10:1-29	☐ 11:1-43	☐ 12:1-33	☐ 13:1-34	☐ 14:1-31
43	☐ 15:1-34	☐ 16:1—17:24	☐ 18:1-46	☐ 19:1-21	☐ 20:1-43	☐ 21:1—22:53	☐ 2 Kings 1:1-18
44	☐ 2:1—3:27	☐ 4:1-44	☐ 5:1—6:33	☐ 7:1-20	☐ 8:1-29	☐ 9:1-37	☐ 10:1-36
45	☐ 11:1—12:21	☐ 13:1—14:29	☐ 15:1-38	☐ 16:1-20	☐ 17:1-41	☐ 18:1-37	☐ 19:1-37
46	☐ 20:1—21:26	☐ 22:1-20	☐ 23:1-37	☐ 24:1—25:30	☐ 1 Chron 1:1-54	☐ 2:1—3:24	☐ 4:1—5:26
47	☐ 6:1-81	☐ 7:1-40	☐ 8:1-40	☐ 9:1-44	☐ 10:1—11:47	☐ 12:1-40	☐ 13:1—14:17
48	☐ 15:1—16:43	☐ 17:1-27	☐ 18:1—19:19	☐ 20:1—21:30	☐ 22:1—23:32	☐ 24:1—25:31	☐ 26:1-32
49	☐ 27:1-34	☐ 28:1—29:30	☐ 2 Chron 1:1-17	☐ 2:1—3:17	☐ 4:1—5:14	☐ 6:1-42	☐ 7:1—8:18
50	☐ 9:1—10:19	☐ 11:1—12:16	☐ 13:1—15:19	☐ 16:1—17:19	☐ 18:1—19:11	☐ 20:1-37	☐ 21:1—22:12
51	☐ 23:1—24:27	☐ 25:1—26:23	☐ 27:1—28:27	☐ 29:1-36	☐ 30:1—31:21	☐ 32:1-33	☐ 33:1—34:33
52	☐ 35:1—36:23	☐ Ezra 1:1-11	☐ 2:1-70	☐ 3:1—4:24	☐ 5:1—6:22	☐ 7:1-28	☐ 8:1-36

Reading Schedule for the Recovery Version of the Old Testament with Footnotes

Wk.	Lord's Day	Monday	Tuesday	Wednesday	Thursday	Friday	Saturday
53	9:1—10:44	Neh 1:1-11	2:1—3:32	4:1—5:19	6:1-19	7:1-73	8:1-18
54	9:1-20	9:21-38	10:1—11:36	12:1-47	13:1-31	Esth 1:1-22	2:1—3:15
55	4:1—5:14	6:1—7:10	8:1-17	9:1—10:3	Job 1:1-22	2:1—3:26	4:1—5:27
56	6:1—7:21	8:1—9:35	10:1—11:20	12:1—13:28	14:1—15:35	16:1—17:16	18:1—19:29
57	20:1—21:34	22:1—23:17	24:1—25:6	26:1—27:23	28:1—29:25	30:1—31:40	32:1—33:33
58	34:1—35:16	36:1-33	37:1-24	38:1-41	39:1-30	40:1-24	41:1-34
59	42:1-17	Psa 1:1-6	2:1—3:8	4:1—6:10	7:1—8:9	9:1—10:18	11:1—15:5
60	16:1—17:15	18:1-50	19:1—21:13	22:1-31	23:1—24:10	25:1—27:14	28:1—30:12
61	31:1—32:11	33:1—34:22	35:1—36:12	37:1-40	38:1—39:13	40:1—41:13	42:1—43:5
62	44:1-26	45:1-17	46:1—48:14	49:1—50:23	51:1—52:9	53:1—55:23	56:1—58:11
63	59:1—61:8	62:1—64:10	65:1—67:7	68:1-35	69:1—70:5	71:1—72:20	73:1—74:23
64	75:1—77:20	78:1-72	79:1—81:16	82:1—84:12	85:1—87:7	88:1—89:52	90:1—91:16
65	92:1—94:23	95:1—97:12	98:1—101:8	102:1—103:22	104:1—105:45	106:1-48	107:1-43
66	108:1—109:31	110:1—112:10	113:1—115:18	116:1—118:29	119:1-32	119:33-72	119:73-120
67	119:121-176	120:1—124:8	125:1—128:6	129:1—132:18	133:1—135:21	136:1—138:8	139:1—140:13
68	141:1—144:15	145:1—147:20	148:1—150:6	Prov 1:1-33	2:1—3:35	4:1—5:23	6:1-35
69	7:1—8:36	9:1—10:32	11:1—12:28	13:1—14:35	15:1-33	16:1-33	17:1-28
70	18:1-24	19:1—20:30	21:1—22:29	23:1-35	24:1—25:28	26:1—27:27	28:1—29:27
71	30:1-33	31:1-31	Eccl 1:1-18	2:1—3:22	4:1—5:20	6:1—7:29	8:1—9:18
72	10:1—11:10	12:1-14	S.S 1:1-8	1:9-17	2:1-17	3:1-11	4:1-8
73	4:9-16	5:1-16	6:1-13	7:1-13	8:1-14	Isa 1:1-11	1:12-31
74	2:1-22	3:1-26	4:1-6	5:1-30	6:1-13	7:1-25	8:1-22
75	9:1-21	10:1-34	11:1—12:6	13:1-22	14:1-14	14:15-32	15:1—16:14
76	17:1—18:7	19:1-25	20:1—21:17	22:1-25	23:1-18	24:1-23	25:1-12
77	26:1—21	27:1-13	28:1-29	29:1-24	30:1-33	31:1—32:20	33:1-24
78	34:1-17	35:1-10	36:1-22	37:1-38	38:1—39:8	40:1-31	41:1-29

Reading Schedule for the Recovery Version of the Old Testament with Footnotes

Wk.	Lord's Day	Monday	Tuesday	Wednesday	Thursday	Friday	Saturday
79	☐ 42:1-25	☐ 43:1-28	☐ 44:1-28	☐ 45:1-25	☐ 46:1-13	☐ 47:1-15	☐ 48:1-22
80	☐ 49:1-13	☐ 49:14-26	☐ 50:1—51:23	☐ 52:1-15	☐ 53:1-12	☐ 54:1-17	☐ 55:1-13
81	☐ 56:1-12	☐ 57:1-21	☐ 58:1-14	☐ 59:1-21	☐ 60:1-22	☐ 61:1-11	☐ 62:1-12
82	☐ 63:1-19	☐ 64:1-12	☐ 65:1-25	☐ 66:1-24	☐ Jer 1:1-19	☐ 2:1-19	☐ 2:20-37
83	☐ 3:1-25	☐ 4:1-31	☐ 5:1-31	☐ 6:1-30	☐ 7:1-34	☐ 8:1-22	☐ 9:1-26
84	☐ 10:1-25	☐ 11:1—12:17	☐ 13:1-27	☐ 14:1-22	☐ 15:1-21	☐ 16:1—17:27	☐ 18:1-23
85	☐ 19:1—20:18	☐ 21:1—22:30	☐ 23:1-40	☐ 24:1—25:38	☐ 26:1—27:22	☐ 28:1—29:32	☐ 30:1-24
86	☐ 31:1-23	☐ 31:24-40	☐ 32:1-44	☐ 33:1-26	☐ 34:1-22	☐ 35:1-19	☐ 36:1-32
87	☐ 37:1-21	☐ 38:1-28	☐ 39:1—40:16	☐ 41:1—42:22	☐ 43:1—44:30	☐ 45:1—46:28	☐ 47:1—48:16
88	☐ 48:17-47	☐ 49:1-22	☐ 49:23-39	☐ 50:1-27	☐ 50:28-46	☐ 51:1-27	☐ 51:28-64
89	☐ 52:1-34	☐ Lam 1:1-22	☐ 2:1-22	☐ 3:1-39	☐ 3:40-66	☐ 4:1-22	☐ 5:1-22
90	☐ Ezek 1:1-14	☐ 1:15-28	☐ 2:1—3:27	☐ 4:1—5:17	☐ 6:1—7:27	☐ 8:1—9:11	☐ 10:1—11:25
91	☐ 12:1—13:23	☐ 14:1—15:8	☐ 16:1-63	☐ 17:1—18:32	☐ 19:1-14	☐ 20:1-49	☐ 21:1-32
92	☐ 22:1-31	☐ 23:1-49	☐ 24:1-27	☐ 25:1—26:21	☐ 27:1-36	☐ 28:1-26	☐ 29:1—30:26
93	☐ 31:1—32:32	☐ 33:1-33	☐ 34:1-31	☐ 35:1—36:21	☐ 36:22-38	☐ 37:1-28	☐ 38:1—39:29
94	☐ 40:1-27	☐ 40:28-49	☐ 41:1-26	☐ 42:1—43:27	☐ 44:1-31	☐ 45:1-25	☐ 46:1-24
95	☐ 47:1-23	☐ 48:1-35	☐ Dan 1:1-21	☐ 2:1-30	☐ 2:31-49	☐ 3:1-30	☐ 4:1-37
96	☐ 5:1-31	☐ 6:1-28	☐ 7:1-12	☐ 7:13-28	☐ 8:1-27	☐ 9:1-27	☐ 10:1-21
97	☐ 11:1-22	☐ 11:23-45	☐ 12:1-13	☐ Hosea 1:1-11	☐ 2:1-23	☐ 3:1—4:19	☐ 5:1-15
98	☐ 6:1-11	☐ 7:1-16	☐ 8:1-14	☐ 9:1-17	☐ 10:1-15	☐ 11:1-12	☐ 12:1-14
99	☐ 13:1—14:9	☐ Joel 1:1-20	☐ 2:1-16	☐ 2:17-32	☐ 3:1-21	☐ Amos 1:1-15	☐ 2:1-16
100	☐ 3:1-15	☐ 4:1—5:27	☐ 6:1—7:17	☐ 8:1—9:15	☐ Obad 1-21	☐ Jonah 1:1-17	☐ 2:1—4:11
101	☐ Micah 1:1-16	☐ 2:1—3:12	☐ 4:1—5:15	☐ 6:1—7:20	☐ Nahum 1:1-15	☐ 2:1—3:19	☐ Hab 1:1-17
102	☐ 2:1-20	☐ 3:1-19	☐ Zeph 1:1-18	☐ 2:1-15	☐ 3:1-20	☐ Hag 1:1-15	☐ 2:1-23
103	☐ Zech 1:1-21	☐ 2:1-13	☐ 3:1-10	☐ 4:1-14	☐ 5:1—6:15	☐ 7:1—8:23	☐ 9:1-17
104	☐ 10:1—11:17	☐ 12:1—13:9	☐ 14:1-21	☐ Mal 1:1-14	☐ 2:1-17	☐ 3:1-18	☐ 4:1-6

Reading Schedule for the Recovery Version of the New Testament with Footnotes

Wk.	Lord's Day	Monday	Tuesday	Wednesday	Thursday	Friday	Saturday
1	☐ Matt 1:1-2	☐ 1:3-7	☐ 1:8-17	☐ 1:18-25	☐ 2:1-23	☐ 3:1-6	☐ 3:7-17
2	☐ 4:1-11	☐ 4:12-25	☐ 5:1-4	☐ 5:5-12	☐ 5:13-20	☐ 5:21-26	☐ 5:27-48
3	☐ 6:1-8	☐ 6:9-18	☐ 6:19-34	☐ 7:1-12	☐ 7:13-29	☐ 8:1-13	☐ 8:14-22
4	☐ 8:23-34	☐ 9:1-13	☐ 9:14-17	☐ 9:18-34	☐ 9:35—10:5	☐ 10:6-25	☐ 10:26-42
5	☐ 11:1-15	☐ 11:16-30	☐ 12:1-14	☐ 12:15-32	☐ 12:33-42	☐ 12:43—13:2	☐ 13:3-12
6	☐ 13:13-30	☐ 13:31-43	☐ 13:44-58	☐ 14:1-13	☐ 14:14-21	☐ 14:22-36	☐ 15:1-20
7	☐ 15:21-31	☐ 15:32-39	☐ 16:1-12	☐ 16:13-20	☐ 16:21-28	☐ 17:1-13	☐ 17:14-27
8	☐ 18:1-14	☐ 18:15-22	☐ 18:23-35	☐ 19:1-15	☐ 19:16-30	☐ 20:1-16	☐ 20:17-34
9	☐ 21:1-11	☐ 21:12-22	☐ 21:23-32	☐ 21:33-46	☐ 22:1-22	☐ 22:23-33	☐ 22:34-46
10	☐ 23:1-12	☐ 23:13-39	☐ 24:1-14	☐ 24:15-31	☐ 24:32-51	☐ 25:1-13	☐ 25:14-30
11	☐ 25:31-46	☐ 26:1-16	☐ 26:17-35	☐ 26:36-46	☐ 26:47-64	☐ 26:65-75	☐ 27:1-26
12	☐ 27:27-44	☐ 27:45-56	☐ 27:57—28:15	☐ 28:16-20	☐ Mark 1:1	☐ 1:2-6	☐ 1:7-13
13	☐ 1:14-28	☐ 1:29-45	☐ 2:1-12	☐ 2:13-28	☐ 3:1-19	☐ 3:20-35	☐ 4:1-25
14	☐ 4:26-41	☐ 5:1-20	☐ 5:21-43	☐ 6:1-29	☐ 6:30-56	☐ 7:1-23	☐ 7:24-37
15	☐ 8:1-26	☐ 8:27—9:1	☐ 9:2-29	☐ 9:30-50	☐ 10:1-16	☐ 10:17-34	☐ 10:35-52
16	☐ 11:1-16	☐ 11:17-33	☐ 12:1-27	☐ 12:28-44	☐ 13:1-13	☐ 13:14-37	☐ 14:1-26
17	☐ 14:27-52	☐ 14:53-72	☐ 15:1-15	☐ 15:16-47	☐ 16:1-8	☐ 16:9-20	☐ Luke 1:1-4
18	☐ 1:5-25	☐ 1:26-46	☐ 1:47-56	☐ 1:57-80	☐ 2:1-8	☐ 2:9-20	☐ 2:21-39
19	☐ 2:40-52	☐ 3:1-20	☐ 3:21-38	☐ 4:1-13	☐ 4:14-30	☐ 4:31-44	☐ 5:1-26
20	☐ 5:27—6:16	☐ 6:17-38	☐ 6:39-49	☐ 7:1-17	☐ 7:18-23	☐ 7:24-35	☐ 7:36-50
21	☐ 8:1-15	☐ 8:16-25	☐ 8:26-39	☐ 8:40-56	☐ 9:1-17	☐ 9:18-26	☐ 9:27-36
22	☐ 9:37-50	☐ 9:51-62	☐ 10:1-11	☐ 10:12-24	☐ 10:25-37	☐ 10:38-42	☐ 11:1-13
23	☐ 11:14-26	☐ 11:27-36	☐ 11:37-54	☐ 12:1-12	☐ 12:13-21	☐ 12:22-34	☐ 12:35-48
24	☐ 12:49-59	☐ 13:1-9	☐ 13:10-17	☐ 13:18-30	☐ 13:31—14:6	☐ 14:7-14	☐ 14:15-24
25	☐ 14:25-35	☐ 15:1-10	☐ 15:11-21	☐ 15:22-32	☐ 16:1-13	☐ 16:14-22	☐ 16:23-31
26	☐ 17:1-19	☐ 17:20-37	☐ 18:1-14	☐ 18:15-30	☐ 18:31-43	☐ 19:1-10	☐ 19:11-27

Reading Schedule for the Recovery Version of the New Testament with Footnotes

Wk.	Lord's Day	Monday	Tuesday	Wednesday	Thursday	Friday	Saturday
27	☐ Luke 19:28-48	☐ 20:1-19	☐ 20:20-38	☐ 20:39—21:4	☐ 21:5-27	☐ 21:28-38	☐ 22:1-20
28	☐ 22:21-38	☐ 22:39-54	☐ 22:55-71	☐ 23:1-43	☐ 23:44-56	☐ 24:1-12	☐ 24:13-35
29	☐ 24:36-53	☐ John 1:1-13	☐ 1:14-18	☐ 1:19-34	☐ 1:35-51	☐ 2:1-11	☐ 2:12-22
30	☐ 2:23—3:13	☐ 3:14-21	☐ 3:22-36	☐ 4:1-14	☐ 4:15-26	☐ 4:27-42	☐ 4:43-54
31	☐ 5:1-16	☐ 5:17-30	☐ 5:31-47	☐ 6:1-15	☐ 6:16-31	☐ 6:32-51	☐ 6:52-71
32	☐ 7:1-9	☐ 7:10-24	☐ 7:25-36	☐ 7:37-52	☐ 7:53—8:11	☐ 8:12-27	☐ 8:28-44
33	☐ 8:45-59	☐ 9:1-13	☐ 9:14-34	☐ 9:35—10:9	☐ 10:10-30	☐ 10:31—11:4	☐ 11:5-22
34	☐ 11:23-40	☐ 11:41-57	☐ 12:1-11	☐ 12:12-24	☐ 12:25-36	☐ 12:37-50	☐ 13:1-11
35	☐ 13:12-30	☐ 13:31-38	☐ 14:1-6	☐ 14:7-20	☐ 14:21-31	☐ 15:1-11	☐ 15:12-27
36	☐ 16:1-15	☐ 16:16-33	☐ 17:1-5	☐ 17:6-13	☐ 17:14-24	☐ 17:25—18:11	☐ 18:12-27
37	☐ 18:28-40	☐ 19:1-16	☐ 19:17-30	☐ 19:31-42	☐ 20:1-13	☐ 20:14-18	☐ 20:19-22
38	☐ 20:23-31	☐ 21:1-14	☐ 21:15-22	☐ 21:23-25	☐ Acts 1:1-8	☐ 1:9-14	☐ 1:15-26
39	☐ 2:1-13	☐ 2:14-21	☐ 2:22-36	☐ 2:37-41	☐ 2:42-47	☐ 3:1-18	☐ 3:19—4:22
40	☐ 4:23-37	☐ 5:1-16	☐ 5:17-32	☐ 5:33-42	☐ 6:1—7:1	☐ 7:2-29	☐ 7:30-60
41	☐ 8:1-13	☐ 8:14-25	☐ 8:26-40	☐ 9:1-19	☐ 9:20-43	☐ 10:1-16	☐ 10:17-33
42	☐ 10:34-48	☐ 11:1-18	☐ 11:19-30	☐ 12:1-25	☐ 13:1-12	☐ 13:13-43	☐ 13:44—14:5
43	☐ 14:6-28	☐ 15:1-12	☐ 15:13-34	☐ 15:35—16:5	☐ 16:6-18	☐ 16:19-40	☐ 17:1-18
44	☐ 17:19-34	☐ 18:1-17	☐ 18:18-28	☐ 19:1-20	☐ 19:21-41	☐ 20:1-12	☐ 20:13-38
45	☐ 21:1-14	☐ 21:15-26	☐ 21:27-40	☐ 22:1-21	☐ 22:22-29	☐ 22:30—23:11	☐ 23:12-15
46	☐ 23:16-30	☐ 23:31—24:21	☐ 24:22—25:5	☐ 25:6-27	☐ 26:1-13	☐ 26:14-32	☐ 27:1-26
47	☐ 27:27—28:10	☐ 28:11-22	☐ 28:23-31	☐ Rom 1:1-2	☐ 1:3-7	☐ 1:8-17	☐ 1:18-25
48	☐ 1:26—2:10	☐ 2:11-29	☐ 3:1-20	☐ 3:21-31	☐ 4:1-12	☐ 4:13-25	☐ 5:1-11
49	☐ 5:12-17	☐ 5:18—6:5	☐ 6:6-11	☐ 6:12-23	☐ 7:1-12	☐ 7:13-25	☐ 8:1-2
50	☐ 8:3-6	☐ 8:7-13	☐ 8:14-25	☐ 8:26-39	☐ 9:1-18	☐ 9:19—10:3	☐ 10:4-15
51	☐ 10:16—11:10	☐ 11:11-22	☐ 11:23-36	☐ 12:1-3	☐ 12:4-21	☐ 13:1-14	☐ 14:1-12
52	☐ 14:13-23	☐ 15:1-13	☐ 15:14-33	☐ 16:1-5	☐ 16:6-24	☐ 16:25-27	☐ 1 Cor 1:1-4

Reading Schedule for the Recovery Version of the New Testament with Footnotes

Wk.	Lord's Day	Monday	Tuesday	Wednesday	Thursday	Friday	Saturday
53	1 Cor 1:5-9 □	1:10-17 □	1:18-31 □	2:1-5 □	2:6-10 □	2:11-16 □	3:1-9 □
54	3:10-13 □	3:14-23 □	4:1-9 □	4:10-21 □	5:1-13 □	6:1-11 □	6:12-20 □
55	7:1-16 □	7:17-24 □	7:25-40 □	8:1-13 □	9:1-15 □	9:16-27 □	10:1-4 □
56	10:5-13 □	10:14-33 □	11:1-6 □	11:7-16 □	11:17-26 □	11:27-34 □	12:1-11 □
57	12:12-22 □	12:23-31 □	13:1-13 □	14:1-12 □	14:13-25 □	14:26-33 □	14:34-40 □
58	15:1-19 □	15:20-28 □	15:29-34 □	15:35-49 □	15:50-58 □	16:1-9 □	16:10-24 □
59	2 Cor 1:1-4 □	1:5-14 □	1:15-22 □	1:23—2:11 □	2:12-17 □	3:1-6 □	3:7-11 □
60	3:12-18 □	4:1-6 □	4:7-12 □	4:13-18 □	5:1-8 □	5:9-15 □	5:16-21 □
61	6:1-13 □	6:14—7:4 □	7:5-16 □	8:1-15 □	8:16-24 □	9:1-15 □	10:1-6 □
62	10:7-18 □	11:1-15 □	11:16-33 □	12:1-10 □	12:11-21 □	13:1-10 □	13:11-14 □
63	Gal 1:1-5 □	1:6-14 □	1:15-24 □	2:1-13 □	2:14-21 □	3:1-4 □	3:5-14 □
64	3:15-22 □	3:23-29 □	4:1-7 □	4:8-20 □	4:21-31 □	5:1-12 □	5:13-21 □
65	5:22-26 □	6:1-10 □	6:11-15 □	6:16-18 □	Eph 1:1-3 □	1:4-6 □	1:7-10 □
66	1:11-14 □	1:15-18 □	1:19-23 □	2:1-5 □	2:6-10 □	2:11-14 □	2:15-18 □
67	2:19-22 □	3:1-7 □	3:8-13 □	3:14-18 □	3:19-21 □	4:1-4 □	4:5-10 □
68	4:11-16 □	4:17-24 □	4:25-32 □	5:1-10 □	5:11-21 □	5:22-26 □	5:27-33 □
69	6:1-9 □	6:10-14 □	6:15-18 □	6:19-24 □	Phil 1:1-7 □	1:8-18 □	1:19-26 □
70	1:27—2:4 □	2:5-11 □	2:12-16 □	2:17-30 □	3:1-6 □	3:7-11 □	3:12-16 □
71	3:17-21 □	4:1-9 □	4:10-23 □	Col 1:1-8 □	1:9-13 □	1:14-23 □	1:24-29 □
72	2:1-7 □	2:8-15 □	2:16-23 □	3:1-4 □	3:5-15 □	3:16-25 □	4:1-18 □
73	1 Thes 1:1-3 □	1:4-10 □	2:1-12 □	2:13—3:5 □	3:6-13 □	4:1-10 □	4:11—5:11 □
74	5:12-28 □	2 Thes 1:1-12 □	2:1-17 □	3:1-18 □	1 Tim 1:1-2 □	1:3-4 □	1:5-14 □
75	1:15-20 □	2:1-7 □	2:8-15 □	3:1-13 □	3:14—4:5 □	4:6-16 □	5:1-25 □
76	6:1-10 □	6:11-21 □	2 Tim 1:1-10 □	1:11-18 □	2:1-15 □	2:16-26 □	3:1-13 □
77	3:14—4:8 □	4:9-22 □	Titus 1:1-4 □	1:5-16 □	2:1-15 □	3:1-8 □	3:9-15 □
78	Philem 1:1-11 □	1:12-25 □	Heb 1:1-2 □	1:3-5 □	1:6-14 □	2:1-9 □	2:10-18 □

Reading Schedule for the Recovery Version of the New Testament with Footnotes

Wk.	Lord's Day	Monday	Tuesday	Wednesday	Thursday	Friday	Saturday
79	Heb 3:1-6 ☐	3:7-19 ☐	4:1-9 ☐	4:10-13 ☐	4:14-16 ☐	5:1-10 ☐	5:11—6:3 ☐
80	6:4-8 ☐	6:9-20 ☐	7:1-10 ☐	7:11-28 ☐	8:1-6 ☐	8:7-13 ☐	9:1-4 ☐
81	9:5-14 ☐	9:15-28 ☐	10:1-18 ☐	10:19-28 ☐	10:29-39 ☐	11:1-6 ☐	11:7-19 ☐
82	11:20-31 ☐	11:32-40 ☐	12:1-2 ☐	12:3-13 ☐	12:14-17 ☐	12:18-26 ☐	12:27-29 ☐
83	13:1-7 ☐	13:8-12 ☐	13:13-15 ☐	13:16-25 ☐	James 1:1-8 ☐	1:9-18 ☐	1:19-27 ☐
84	2:1-13 ☐	2:14-26 ☐	3:1-18 ☐	4:1-10 ☐	4:11-17 ☐	5:1-12 ☐	5:13-20 ☐
85	1 Pet 1:1-2 ☐	1:3-4 ☐	1:5 ☐	1:6-9 ☐	1:10-12 ☐	1:13-17 ☐	1:18-25 ☐
86	2:1-3 ☐	2:4-8 ☐	2:9-17 ☐	2:18-25 ☐	3:1-13 ☐	3:14-22 ☐	4:1-6 ☐
87	4:7-16 ☐	4:17-19 ☐	5:1-4 ☐	5:5-9 ☐	5:10-14 ☐	2 Pet 1:1-2 ☐	1:3-4 ☐
88	1:5-8 ☐	1:9-11 ☐	1:12-18 ☐	1:19-21 ☐	2:1-3 ☐	2:4-11 ☐	2:12-22 ☐
89	3:1-6 ☐	3:7-9 ☐	3:10-12 ☐	3:13-15 ☐	3:16 ☐	3:17-18 ☐	1 John 1:1-2 ☐
90	1:3-4 ☐	1:5 ☐	1:6 ☐	1:7 ☐	1:8-10 ☐	2:1-2 ☐	2:3-11 ☐
91	2:12-14 ☐	2:15-19 ☐	2:20-23 ☐	2:24-27 ☐	2:28-29 ☐	3:1-5 ☐	3:6-10 ☐
92	3:11-18 ☐	3:19-24 ☐	4:1-6 ☐	4:7-11 ☐	4:12-15 ☐	4:16—5:3 ☐	5:4-13 ☐
93	5:14-17 ☐	5:18-21 ☐	2 John 1:1-3 ☐	1:4-9 ☐	1:10-13 ☐	3 John 1:1-6 ☐	1:7-14 ☐
94	Jude 1:1-4 ☐	1:5-10 ☐	1:11-19 ☐	1:20-25 ☐	Rev 1:1-3 ☐	1:4-6 ☐	1:7-11 ☐
95	1:12-13 ☐	1:14-16 ☐	1:17-20 ☐	2:1-6 ☐	2:7 ☐	2:8-9 ☐	2:10-11 ☐
96	2:12-14 ☐	2:15-17 ☐	2:18-23 ☐	2:24-29 ☐	3:1-3 ☐	3:4-6 ☐	3:7-9 ☐
97	3:10-13 ☐	3:14-18 ☐	3:19-22 ☐	4:1-5 ☐	4:6-7 ☐	4:8-11 ☐	5:1-6 ☐
98	5:7-14 ☐	6:1-8 ☐	6:9-17 ☐	7:1-8 ☐	7:9-17 ☐	8:1-6 ☐	8:7-12 ☐
99	8:13—9:11 ☐	9:12-21 ☐	10:1-4 ☐	10:5-11 ☐	11:1-4 ☐	11:5-14 ☐	11:15-19 ☐
100	12:1-4 ☐	12:5-9 ☐	12:10-18 ☐	13:1-10 ☐	13:11-18 ☐	14:1-5 ☐	14:6-12 ☐
101	14:13-20 ☐	15:1-8 ☐	16:1-12 ☐	16:13-21 ☐	17:1-6 ☐	17:7-18 ☐	18:1-8 ☐
102	18:9—19:4 ☐	19:5-10 ☐	19:11-16 ☐	19:17-21 ☐	20:1-6 ☐	20:7-10 ☐	20:11-15 ☐
103	21:1 ☐	21:2 ☐	21:3-8 ☐	21:9-13 ☐	21:14-18 ☐	21:19-21 ☐	21:22-27 ☐
104	22:1 ☐	22:2 ☐	22:3-11 ☐	22:12-15 ☐	22:16-17 ☐	22:18-21 ☐	

Week 1 — Day 4　　　　Today's verses

Psa. Great is Jehovah, and much to be praised
48:1-2 in the city of our God, in His holy mountain. Beautiful in elevation, the joy of the whole earth, is Mount Zion, the sides of the north, the city of the great King.

Date

Week 1 — Day 1　　　　Today's verses

Luke And He said to them, These are My words
24:44 which I spoke to you while I was still with you, that all the things written in the Law of Moses and the Prophets and Psalms concerning Me must be fulfilled.

Psa. But I have installed My King upon Zion,
2:6-7 My holy mountain. I will recount the decree of Jehovah; He said to Me: You are My Son; today I have begotten You.

Date

Week 1 — Day 5　　　　Today's verses

Psa. All the ends of the earth will remember
22:27-29 and return to Jehovah, and all families of the nations will worship before You; for the kingdom is Jehovah's, and He rules among the nations. All the flourishing of the earth will eat and worship...

Date

Week 1 — Day 2　　　　Today's verses

Psa. What is mortal man, that You remember
8:4-6 him, and the son of man, that You visit him? You have made Him a little lower than angels and have crowned Him with glory and honor. For You have caused Him to rule over the works of Your hands; You have put all things under His feet.

Date

Week 1 — Day 6　　　　Today's verses

Psa. O Jehovah our Lord, how excellent is
8:1-2 Your name in all the earth, You who have set Your glory over the heavens! Out of the mouths of babes and sucklings You have established strength because of Your adversaries, to stop the enemy and the avenger.
9 O Jehovah our Lord, how excellent is Your name in all the earth!

Date

Week 1 — Day 3　　　　Today's verses

Psa. One thing I have asked from Jehovah; that
27:4 do I seek: to dwell in the house of Jehovah all the days of my life, to behold the beauty of Jehovah, and to inquire in His temple.

84:1 How lovely are Your tabernacles, O Jehovah of hosts!

Date

Week 2 — Day 4   Today's verses

Psa. I will recount the decree of Jehovah; He
2:7-9 said to Me: You are My Son; today I have
        begotten You. Ask of Me, and I will give
        the nations as Your inheritance and the
        limits of the earth as Your possession. You
        will break them with an iron rod; You will
        shatter them like a potter's vessel.

_____
Date

Week 2 — Day 5   Today's verses

Psa. Now therefore, O kings, be prudent; take
2:10-12 the admonition, O judges of the earth.
        Serve Jehovah with fear, and rejoice with
        trembling. Kiss the Son lest He be angry
        and you perish from the way; for His
        anger may suddenly be kindled. Blessed
        are all those who take refuge in Him.

_____
Date

Week 2 — Day 6   Today's verses

Psa. O Jehovah, cause me to know my end,
39:4-5 and the measure of my days, what it is.
        May I know how transient I am. Behold,
        You have made my days as *mere hand-
        breadths*, and my lifetime is as nothing
        before You; surely every man at his best is
        altogether vanity. Selah

Eph. Peace to the brothers and love with faith
6:23 from God the Father and the Lord Jesus
        Christ.

_____
Date

Week 2 — Day 1   Today's verses

Col. Who is the image of the invisible God, the
1:15 Firstborn of all creation.
18-19 And He is the Head of the Body, the
        church; He is the beginning, the Firstborn
        from the dead, that He Himself might
        have the first place in all things; for in Him
        all the fullness was pleased to dwell.

_____
Date

Week 2 — Day 2   Today's verses

Psa. The kings of the earth take their stand, and
2:2, 4 the rulers sit in counsel together, against
        Jehovah and against His Anointed:…He
        who sits in the heavens laughs; the Lord
        has them in derision.

_____
Date

Week 2 — Day 3   Today's verses

Psa. But I have installed My King upon Zion,
2:6 My holy mountain.
Heb. But you have come forward to Mount
12:22 Zion and to the city of the living God, the
        heavenly Jerusalem; and to myriads of an-
        gels, to the universal gathering.

_____
Date

Week 3 — Day 4 Today's verses

Psa. You have made Him a little lower than an-
8:5-8 gels and have crowned Him with glory
and honor. For You have caused Him to
rule over the works of Your hands; You
have put all things under His feet: all
sheep and oxen, as well as the beasts of
the field the birds of heaven and the fish of
the sea, whatever passes through the
paths of the seas.

Date

Week 3 — Day 5 Today's verses

1 Cor. ...The lowborn things of the world and
1:28-30 the despised things God has chosen,
things which are not, that He might bring
to nought the things which are, so that no
flesh may boast before God. But of Him
you are in Christ Jesus, who became wisdom to us from God: both righteousness
and sanctification and redemption.

Date

Week 3 — Day 6 Today's verses

Psa. O Jehovah our Lord, how excellent is
8:9 Your name in all the earth!
Matt. You then pray in this way: Our Father who
6:9-10 is in the heavens, Your name be sanctified; Your kingdom come; Your will be
done, as in heaven, so also on earth.

Date

Week 3 — Day 1 Today's verses

Heb. ..."What is man, that You bring him to
2:6-9 mind? Or the son of man, that You care for
him? You have made Him a little inferior
to the angels; You have crowned Him
with glory and honor and have set Him
over the works of Your hands; You have
subjected all things under His feet."...But
now we do not yet see all things subjected
to Him, but we see Jesus, who was made a
little inferior to the angels because of the
suffering of death, crowned with glory
and honor...

Date

Week 3 — Day 2 Today's verses

Psa. Out of the mouths of babes and sucklings
8:2 You have established strength because of
Your adversaries, to stop the enemy and
the avenger.
Matt. ...And Jesus said to them, Yes. Have you
21:16 never read, "Out of the mouth of infants
and sucklings You have perfected praise"?

Date

Week 3 — Day 3 Today's verses

Psa. When I see Your heavens, the works of
8:3-4 Your fingers, the moon and the stars,
which You have ordained, what is mortal
man, that You remember him, and the son
of man, that You visit him?
Gen. And God said, Let Us make man in Our
1:26 image, according to Our likeness; and let
them have dominion over the fish of the
sea and over the birds of heaven and over
the cattle and over all the earth and over
every creeping thing that creeps upon the
earth.

Date

Week 4 — Day 1 Today's verses

Psa. 15:1 O Jehovah, who may sojourn in Your tent? Who may dwell on Your holy mountain?

Matt. 17:5 While he was still speaking, behold, a bright cloud overshadowed them, and behold, a voice out of the cloud, saying, This is My Son, the Beloved, in whom I have found My delight. Hear Him!

_____
Date

Week 4 — Day 2 Today's verses

Psa. 16:1-4 Preserve me, O God, for I take refuge in You. I say to Jehovah, You are my Lord; no good have I beyond You; as for the saints who are on the earth, they are the excellent; all my delight is in them. The sorrows of them who bartered for some other god will be multiplied; their drink offerings of blood I will not offer, nor will I take up their names upon my lips.

_____
Date

Week 4 — Day 3 Today's verses

Psa. 16:5-8 Jehovah is the portion of my inheritance and of my cup; You maintain my lot. The measuring lines have fallen on pleasant places for me; indeed the inheritance is beautiful to me. I will bless Jehovah, who counsels me; indeed in the nights my inward parts instruct me. I have set Jehovah before me continually; because He is at my right hand, I shall not be shaken.

_____
Date

Week 4 — Day 4 Today's verses

Acts 2:25-27 For David says regarding Him, "I saw the Lord continually before me, because He is on my right hand, that I may not be shaken. Therefore my heart was made glad and my tongue exulted; moreover, also my flesh will rest in hope, because You will not abandon my soul to Hades, nor will You permit Your Holy One to see corruption."

_____
Date

Week 4 — Day 5 Today's verses

Psa. 16:10-11 For You will not abandon my soul to Sheol, nor let Your Holy One see the pit. You will make known to me the path of life; in Your presence is fullness of joy; at Your right hand there are pleasures forever.

Acts 2:28 "You have made known to me the ways of life; You will make me full of gladness with Your presence."

Phil. 2:9 Therefore also God highly exalted Him and bestowed on Him the name which is above every name.

_____
Date

Week 4 — Day 6 Today's verses

Psa. 15:1 O Jehovah, who may sojourn in Your tent? Who may dwell on Your holy mountain?

16:11 ...In Your presence is fullness of joy; at Your right hand there are pleasures forever.

_____
Date

Week 5 — Day 4   Today's verses

Heb. For both He who sanctifies and those who
2:11-12 are being sanctified are all of One, for
which cause He is not ashamed to call
them brothers, saying, "I will declare Your
name to My brothers; in the midst of the
church I will sing hymns of praise to You."

Date

Week 5 — Day 5   Today's verses

Psa. I will declare Your name to my brothers;
22:22 in the midst of the assembly I will praise
You.

Rom. Because those whom He foreknew, He
8:29 also predestinated *to be* conformed to the
image of His Son, that He might be the
Firstborn among many brothers.

Date

Week 5 — Day 6   Today's verses

Psa. For the kingdom is Jehovah's, and He
22:28 rules among the nations.
30 A seed will serve Him; that which concerns the Lord will be told to a *coming*
generation.

Date

Week 5 — Day 1   Today's verses

Luke ...Behold we are going up to Jerusalem,
18:31-33 and all things which have been written
through the prophets regarding the Son of
Man will be accomplished, for He will be
delivered up to the Gentiles and will be
mocked and outrageously treated and
spat upon; and when they have scourged
Him, they will kill Him; and on the third
day He will rise.

Date

Week 5 — Day 2   Today's verses

Psa. My strength is dried up like a shard, and
22:15 my tongue is stuck to my jaws; You have
put me in the dust of death.

2 Cor. Him who did not know sin He made sin
5:21 on our behalf that we might become the
righteousness of God in Him.

Date

Week 5 — Day 3   Today's verses

Psa. My God, my God, why have You forsaken
22:1 me? *Why are You* so far from saving me,
from the words of my groaning?

Heb. ...Through His own blood, entered once
9:12 for all into the *Holy of* Holies, obtaining
an eternal redemption.

14 How much more will the blood of Christ,
who through the eternal Spirit offered
Himself without blemish to God, purify
our conscience from dead works to serve
the living God?

Date

Week 6 — Day 6   **Today's verses**

Psa. Surely goodness and lovingkindness will
23:6 follow me all the days of my life, and I will
dwell in the house of Jehovah for the
length of *my* days.

27:4 One thing I have asked from Jehovah; that
do I seek: to dwell in the house of Jehovah
all the days of my life, to behold the
beauty of Jehovah, and to inquire in His
temple.

Week 6 — Day 5   **Today's verses**

Psa. You spread a table before me in the pres-
23:5 ence of my adversaries; You anoint my
head with oil; my cup runs over.

133:2 It is like the fine oil upon the head that ran
down upon the beard, upon Aaron's
beard, that ran down upon the hem of his
garments.

1 Cor. The cup of blessing which we bless, is
10:16 it not the fellowship of the blood of
Christ?...

Week 6 — Day 4   **Today's verses**

Psa. Even though I walk through the valley of
23:4 the shadow of death, I do not fear evil, for
You are with me; Your rod and Your staff,
they comfort me.

2 Tim. The Lord be with your spirit. Grace be
4:22 with you.

Week 6 — Day 3   **Today's verses**

Psa. ...He leads me beside waters of rest. He
23:2-3 restores my soul; He guides me on the
paths of righteousness for His name's
sake.

John He who believes into Me...out of his in-
7:38-39 nermost being shall flow rivers of living
water. But this He said concerning the
Spirit...

Week 6 — Day 2   **Today's verses**

Psa. Jehovah is my Shepherd; I will lack noth-
23:1-2 ing. He makes me lie down in green pastures; He leads me beside waters of rest.

John I am the door; if anyone enters through
10:9 Me, he shall be saved and shall go in and
go out and shall find pasture.

11 I am the good Shepherd; the good Shepherd lays down His life for the sheep.

Week 6 — Day 1   **Today's verses**

John He said to him again a second time, Simon,
21:16 *son* of John, do you love Me?...Shepherd
My sheep.

1 Pet. For you were like sheep being led astray,
2:25 but you have now returned to the Shepherd and Overseer of your souls.

5:2,4 Shepherd the flock of God among
you...And when the Chief Shepherd is
manifested, you will receive the unfading
crown of glory.